Andrew Patton Happer

Is The Shang-ti Of The Chinese Classics The Same Being As Jehovah Of The Sacred Scriptures? ..

Andrew Patton Happer

Is The Shang-ti Of The Chinese Classics The Same Being As Jehovah Of The Sacred Scriptures? ..

ISBN/EAN: 9783337115692

Printed in Europe, USA, Canada, Australia, Japan

Cover: Foto ©Lupo / pixelio.de

More available books at **www.hansebooks.com**

上帝

PART I,

Is the Shang-Ti of the Chinese Classics the same Being as Jehovah of the Sacred Scriptures?

PART II,

What Being is Designated Shang-Ti in the Chinese Classics and in the Ritual of the State Religion of China.

BY

INQUIRER.

A. P. Happer

SHANGHAI:
PRESBYTERIAN MISSION PRESS.
MDCCCLXXVII.

TO THE DIRECTORS AND OFFICERS, OF THE MISSIONARY, BIBLE AND TRACT SOCIETIES OF GERMANY, GREAT BRITAIN AND AMERICA, WHO ARE CO-OPERATING IN THE EFFORTS FOR THE EVANGELIZATION OF THE EMPIRE OF CHINA; AND TO THE MISSIONARIES WHO ARE LABORING AMONG THIS PEOPLE:

Dear Brethren :—

It is with unfeigned diffidence, that I address these lines to you. The unexpected favor with which my former article on the meaning of "Shin" was received by many, and other circumstances, led me to continue my inquiries. In the prosecution thereof, I have arrived at some conclusions which I regard as of great importance, and therefore venture to present them to you for your consideration.

Formerly it was considered by some of those who were engaged in translating the Sacred Scriptures into Chinese, that Shangti was a common name which could be applied, with more or less propriety, to all objects of worship. It has been so used by some in the translation of the Bible into this language. But the Rev. Dr. Legge, formerly missionary at Hongkong, and now the Professor of Chinese at Oxford, has shown with a conclusiveness that utterly precludes all further discussion on that point, in his translation of the Shoo King and the Shi King, that Shangti *is the name of a distinct* and *individual Being*, who has been worshipped in China for more than four thousand years, and *that Heaven is the synonym of Shangti in designating that Being*. Dr. Legge also maintains with great ability, that the Being called Shangti is the same as Jehovah of the Sacred Scriptures.

In Part I, of this pamphlet, I have given the reasons, drawn from various sources, which show that Shangti *is not the same Being* as Jehovah. In the second Part I have presented the evidence drawn from the Chinese classics and other standard writers, from the ritual of the State religion of China, from Imperial Edicts and prayers, that the great object of Chinese worship is *deified Heaven;* and that Shangti is the designation of this deified object. Hence it follows that Shangti is *the name of a false God*.

It is this last stated fact, which I consider to be of great importance to all who are engaged in the efforts for the evangelization of this populous country. For the *proper* and *distinctive* name of one Being cannot properly be applied to any other Being. And so far as I know, it has never happened hitherto, in the dissemination of the Gospel, that the name of a *false God* has become the standard or distinctive name of Jehovah in the language of any people.

The question which now presses for consideration and decision is this, can *the name* of a particular Being, which is extensively worshipped and which is the great object of worship in the State religion of this Empire, be used as the translation of Elohim in translating the Sacred Scriptures into the language of this people? Praying that "the spirit of a sound mind and of an understanding heart" may be given unto all who are called to consider this question,

I remain, with great respect and esteem for you all,

Yours in Christian love.

INQUIRER.

PART I,

Is the Shang-Ti of the Chinese Classics the same Being as Jehovah of the Sacred Scriptures.

By INQUIRER.

ONE of the most important questions that can engage the minds of missionaries at the present time is this; is the Shangti of the Chinese Classics, the same Being as Jehovah of the Sacred Scriptures? This question is not only important in itself, but it is still more important from its connection with other questions which press for settlement. But little further progress can be made in determining what word shall be used in the translation of Elohim and Theos into Chinese, until this preliminary question shall have been decided. Every one can see, that if Shangti of the Chinese Classics is *indeed* the same Being as Jehovah of the Bible, what an immense vantage ground this gives us as missionaries in our efforts to introduce the Bible and its doctrines amongst this people. So also, if it can be established that Shangti is the same as Jehovah, then there is an end to all further controversy in regard to the distinctive name for God. For if from time immemorial, Jehovah has been called in the language of this people, Shangti, why should we, who bring to them a revelation from Jehovah, seek any other name by which to designate him than that by which he has been so long known to them? But in a matter of so much importance and of such extended relations, we may not receive such a statement as true, on slight or insufficient grounds. The consequences of an error here would be most serious and long continued.

The affirmative of this question has been argued with great ability and learning by the Rev. J. Legge D.D., LL.D., formerly a distinguished missionary at Hongkong, and now the learned Professor of Chinese at Oxford. The statement of his opinion on this subject was first published in a series of letters to the "Hongkong Register," in 1849, and then in 1852, in a book entitled "The Notions of the Chinese Concerning God and Spirits:" and recently, in his paper which was read before, the General Missionary Conference at Shanghai on May 11th, 1877, on "Confucianism in relation to Christianity." The ability and learning displayed in these publications are acknowledged by all; and all will readily admit the clearness and courage with which the learned professor states his opinions. On page 23 of the "Notions of the Chinese" the Dr. says; "My thesis is that the Chinese have a knowledge of the true God, and that the highest Being whom they worship is indeed the same whom we worship." After presenting the argument, in proof of this opinion, and expressing his opinion of Shangti, he says: "I am confident the Christian world will agree with me in saying "this God is our God." The explicit statement thus made by a Christian missionary and a learned scholar, that he regards the chief god of a heathen people, to be the same Being as the God revealed to mankind in the Bible, is sufficiently startling as to challenge investigation. This opinion is so contrary to the opinions on that subject which have been held by Christian men of all ages and countries, that it must be substantiated by very clear proofs before it can be received as true. The Jews regarded the chief gods of all the nations around them, whatever were the titles and attributes ascribed to them, as false gods. The histories of the ancient nations of Egypt, Assyria, Babylon, India and Greece have spoken of the gods of these nations as false gods, hence it would be surpassingly strange and at the same time most interesting, if, while all the other nations of the world within a few hundred years after the deluge had all formed to themselves gods after their own imagination, it should be found that the Chinese have preserved the knowledge of the one living and true God through the long period of more than four thousand years. I have given the subject very careful and patient investigation and at the conclusion of it, I must declare, that after the consideration of all the professor's arguments, I cannot receive the opinion which he supports. The arguments which he presents in support of the opinion that Shangti is the same Being as Jehovah entirely fail to establish their indentity. And the arguments on the other side, in my judgment, make it clear beyond all doubt that Shangti is not the same Being as Jehovah.

I will now present to my readers the arguments, which, in my judgment, establish the opinion that Shangti is not the same as Jehovah. These will be arranged under three heads. 1st, It is contrary to the teachings of the Bible that they are the same Being. 2nd, That the chief gods of the other heathen nations have had attributes and worship, which belong to Jehovah, ascribed to them, as they have been ascribed to Shangti. And 3rd, Shangti is destitute of some of the *essential* attributes and work which belong to Jehovah, and, therefore, he is not the same Being.

1st, This opinion is contrary to the teaching of the word of God. The Bible teaches that *all men* had corrupted their way before Jehovah, and had made unto themselves gods after their own vain thoughts. This is taught in many different ways, both by indirect implication and inferences, and by positive statements. In the Old Testament the implied teachings is, that as all nations had gone away from Jehovah the true God, and made for themselves false gods, the only way of preserving a knowledge of the true God among men was to call a chosen people from among men to whom the knowledge of Jehovah was again made known by special revelation and this knowledge was committed to them as a special trust for preservation. Thus throughout the whole of the Old Testament history, all the nations, with whom the Jews came in contact—such as the various nations of Canaan, the Egyptians, the Assyrians, the Babylonians, &c., worshipped false gods—each nations had its own chief god—as Baal, Ashtoroth, Chemosh, Osiris, &c., in contradistinction to Jehovah the God of the Israelites.

So in the New Testament, wherever the apostles went in preaching the Gospel, in fulfilment of the command of their ascended Lord—to "go into all the world and preach the Gospel to every creature" the people are spoken of as idolaters, worshippers of false gods, and the obvious teaching of the whole narrative, is that the whole world was in the same condition of ignorance of the one living and true God. It would be easy to quote many writers to show that such has been the wide spread and prevailing opinion of Christians of all ages, as to the condition of the nations that had not yet received the written revelation of Jehovah as made in the Bible. But it is hardly necessary to quote testimony to an opinion of such general currency. One may suffice. The late M. L' Abbe Huc, in his work, "History of Christianity in China, &c., &c.," writes thus in a note. "It is not without surprise that we find in the writings of this learned Jesuit [Father Le Comte], such propositions as the following:—'The people of China have preserved for more than 2000 years the knowledge of the true God, and have paid him homage in a manner that might serve as an example to Christians.' Another [Jesuit], too, in speaking of Confucius says;—'His humility and modesty might give grounds for conjecture, that he was not merely a philosopher formed by reason, but *a man inspired by God*, for the reform of this new world.' Father Le Comte was doubtless inspired by a great desire to facilitate the conversion of the Chinese, and especially the literati, but, in the words of the modern apologist of the Society of Jesus, we must say, that in this instance, Christian charity, and the enthusiasm of science, led the Jesuits astray." Crétinean Joly, vol. iii, p. 178, quoted in Huc, vol. iii, p. 247.

The positive statements of the Sacred Scriptures are equally as clear and decided on this point, as the general implications and inferences of the sacred narratives—Joshua says to the children of Israel, after they had entered into the promised land—"Thus saith Jehovah, the God of Israel, your fathers dwelt on the other side of the flood in old time, even Terah, the father of Abraham and the father of Nachor: and they served other gods. Now, therefore, fear Jehovah, and serve him in sincerity and truth: and put away the gods which your fathers served on the other side of the flood, and in Egypt, and serve ye Jehovah." Josh. 24! 3, 11. "Neither shall ye make mention of their gods, nor cause to swear by them." Josh. 28-7. "And the servants of the king of Assyria, said unto him, their gods are gods of the hills; therefore are they stronger than we." Kings, 20: 23. "Hath any of the gods of the nations delivered at all his land out of the hand of the king of Assyria? Where are the gods of Hamoth, and of Arssud? Where are the gods of Sepharvaim, Hena and Ivah? Have they delivered Samaria out of my hand? Who are they among all the gods of the countries that have delivered their country out of mine hand? That Jehovah should deliver Jerusalem out of my hand." II, Kings 18 : 33, 35. "Also Cyrus, the king, brought forth the vessels of the house of Jehovah which Nebuchadnezzar had brought forth out of Jerusalem, and had put them in the house of his gods?" Ezra. 1 : 7. "Hath a nation changed its gods, which are yet no gods?" Jer. 2: 11. These passages all clearly teach that every nation had distinctively its own gods, which each nation respectively worshipped and trusted in.

"Jehovah looked down from heaven upon the children of men to see if there were any that did understand, and did seek God. They are all gone aside, they are all together filthy; there are none that doeth good, no, not one." Ps. 14: 2, 3. "Blessed is the nation whose God is Jehovah; and the people whom he hath chosen for his inheritance. Jehovah looketh from heaven, he beholdeth all the sons of men. From the place of his habitation he looketh upon all the inhabitants of the earth. Ps. 33: 12-14. "Declare his glory among the heathen, his wonders among all people. For Jehovah is great and greatly to be praised; he is to be feared above all gods. For all the gods of the nations are idols but Jehovah made the heavens." Ps. 96: 3-5. This positive and absolute statement, that all the gods of the nations are idols, can only be set aside by a supposition that the reference is not *to all* the nations of the whole world, but only to those nations near to Judea. But any such supposition is precluded by the preceding context where the reference is so wide and universal. And the passages might be indefinitely multiplied showing the universality of the meaning of such expressions in the Psalms. The words are not spoken by a man of his own motion, but by the inspiration of God, to whose omniscient eye the condition of all nations and the objects of their worship were always present. Calvin remarks on this passage. "The people of God were at that time called to maintain a conflict of no inconsiderable or common description with the hosts and prodigious mass of superstitions, which then filled *the whole world*, every country had its own gods peculiar to itself, but these were not unknown in other parts, and it was the true God which was robbed of the glory which belonged to him"—Calvin, Com. on Ps. Vol. IV. On Ps. 14; 2, 3, Calvin says:—"That the interpretation is more appropriate, which supposes that men are here condemned as guilty of a detestable revolt, inasmuch as they are estranged from God." Com. on Ps. Vol. I. Alexander says: "Total and universal corruption could not be more clearly expressed than by the accumulation of the strongest terms, in which, as Luther well observes, the Psalmist, not content with saying *all*, adds, *together*, and then negatively, *no, not one*. The *whole*, not merely all the individuals as such, but the entire race as a totality or ideal person. *The whole (race) has departed*, not merely from the right way, *but from God* instead of seeking him, as intimated in v. 4. *Together*, not merely altogether, or without exception; but in union and by one decisive act or event." Alexander, Com. on Ps. Vol. I.

The declarations of the New Testament are equally clear and explicit. Paul in addressing the idolaters at Lystra, says: "We preach unto you that you should turn from these vanities unto the living God, who made heaven, and earth, and the sea, and all the things that are therein. Who in times past suffered *all nations* to walk in *their own way*. Acts. 14: 16. The same apostle addressing the Athenians, who were so given to the worship of false gods, says;" "The times of this ignorance God winked at: but now he commandeth all men every where to repent." Acts. 17, 30. This same apostle in writing to the Romans, speaking of the Gentiles, which term was used to include *all nations* other than the Jews, writes.—"And changed the glory of the uncorruptible God into an image made like to corruptible man, * * * who changed the truth of God into a lie, and worshipped and served the creature more than the Creator, and even as they did not like to retain God in their knowledge, God gave them over to a reprobate mind, &c." Rom. 1: 23, 25, 28. Alexander on Acts, explains v. 16 of chap. 14, "All nations, *i. e.* all but one, to whom he granted an exclusive revelation. It is therefore equivalent to *all the gentiles*." On verse 30 of chap. 17, he says:—"A thought to be supplied between the verses is, that this degradation and denial of the Godhead had been practised universally for ages, *i. e.* in the whole heathen worship and mythology—*all (men) every where*, a double expression of the universality of the command, made still more striking in the Greek by the use of two cognate terms, which might be *englished*, everybody everywhere." Dr. Lange in com. on this passage says: that "the Greek words express the conception of *universality* in the most explicit manners." The sin must have been as extensive as the commanded repentance. Barnes in his Com. on Roms. on v. 2, 5, chap. i, says:—"The phrase the 'truth of God' is a Hebrew phrase, meaning *the true God*; into a lie *i. e.* into idols or false gods. 'The creature,' created things, as the sun, moon, animals, &c." Hodge on Rom. explains creature in the same way, "not creation but any particular created thing." Hodge also remarks on v. 24,—"this abandonment of the heathen to the dominion of sin is represented as a punitive infliction. They forsook God wherefore also he gave them up to uncleanness." The sin which the apostle refers to is idolatry. It is admitted by all writers that the Chinese nation have in themselves suffered all the punishment which the apostle states as the punishment of this sin. For a full discussion of the whole subject see Dr. Lelands "Advantage and Necessity of Revelation," and Tholucks "Nature and Moral Influence of Heathenism." Paul in his Epis. to the Thes. says; "Not in the lust of concupiscence even as the gentiles who know not God;" and in the Epis. to the Gal. he writes: "Howbeit then, when ye know not God, ye did service unto them which be no gods" chap. 4, 8. The great apostle of the gentiles, who was ever ready to become "all things to all men that he might save some," whether addressing the literati of Athens, or writing to those at Imperial Rome, declares them all to be idolaters and without the knowledge of the true God, Jehovah. I think that those who receive the Bible as the revelation of God will consider these passages of Scripture to warrant the language of Calvin when he says that the conflict of the people of God is "with the hosts, and prodigious mass of superstition which then *filled the whole world;*" and the expression of the same idea by Alexander when he says; "that this degradation and denial of the Godhead had been practised universally for ages, *i. e. in the whole heathen worship and mythology;*" and that they utterly preclude the supposition that during these 4000 years, the Chinese people have retained the knowledge of the one true God, Jehovah, under the designation of Shangti.

2nd, But the learned professor, the Rev. Dr. Legge, presents as his strongest argument in proof that Shangti is the same being as Jehovah, the fact, that in the Chinese classics and liturgies, so many of the attributes and works which properly belong to Jehovah are ascribed to Shangti. I proceed to consider this argument. The essence of all false religions consists in ascribing the attributes, works, and worship of the true God to some false god. In the very nature of idolatry then, there *must be* the ascription of some of the attributes and works of Jehovah to every false god that is worshipped. It must be predicated of false gods that there are omnipresent, or how can they hear prayers which are offered at different places; that they are omniscient, or how can they know the hearts of those who pray to them; that they are omnipotent, or how can they help those who seek their aid; that they are the rulers over the affairs of men, or how would it pertain to them to attend to the requests of men, that they are merciful and beneficent, or else what ground to hope for their help, and so on as to many other attributes of the true God. It is, therefore, utterly incorrect to say, that the ascription of attributes to any specified being, which properly belong only to Jehovah, is a proof that *that* Being is Jehovah. We must know that the said Being is *really* Jehovah, and then such ascription of the attributes of Jehovah to him is right and proper: but if the specified being is *not* Jehovah, then the ascription of *all* the attributes that properly belong to Jehovah only make it a more flagrant case of *false* worship and homage. In the celebrated case of the claimant to the Tichbourne estates, he had sufficient resemblance to the true heir, and sufficient knowledge of the heir's home life, school days, and early friends as to deceive the mother and many acquaintances; but when this case of resemblance was submitted to rigid investigation and the tests that decide the matter of real *identity*, it was manifest to the greater portion of impartial and discriminating minds, that there was only a resemblance and not true identity. Thus also through the able argumentation of the learned Doctor there is a sufficient degree of resemblance presented to convince some minds that Shangti is the same Being as Jehovah, and to confuse others; but I trust that in the inquiry for the truth, it will be made clear to all, that Shangti is *not* the same Being as Jehovah, who is God over all.

The latest results of the best scholarship, and the widest research into the history of ancient nations, have made known the fact—that to a very large extent, the doctrines of religion, which were made known to the early patriarchs, were transmitted among all nations after the dispersion from Babel. The interesting paper which was prepared by the Rev. John Chalmers, A. M. for the last International Congress of Orientalists, and which was published in the "China Review" for March and April, 1877, shows, how largely this knowledge of the nature and character of God has been transmitted by tradition at first, and subsequently, by written records amongst the Chinese—as the Chinese records have come down to the present time, in a greater number than those of any of the other ancient nations, it is but reasonable that it is possible to compile so full a statement of "The Chinese Natural Theology." The literature on this subject, as regards other nations is abundant and valuable, such as the writings of Wilson and Müller on the religions of India: Wilkinson and Bunsen on those of Egypt: Rawlinson and Layard on Assyria: Adams and Smith on the Antiquities of Greece and Rome: Maurice's Lectures on the Religions of the World, Hardwick's Christ and other masters; Moffat's comparative History of Religions, Gillett's, God in Human Thought, Tyler's Theology of the Greek Poets, and various other authors. The statements made by these various authors, make it clear that among all the early nations there existed, to a wonderful extent, exalted ideas and conceptions of the nature, attributes, and works of God.—They also make it clear, that while all the nations forgot Jehovah, they adopted some particular being as the chief god of their respective countries, and assigned the attributes and works, which belong only to Jehovah, to this imaginary being.

Bunsen in his God in History, thus gives the character of Osiris, one of the chief gods of Egypt.—"Some say Osiris represented the sun; others the Nile—Osiris is the lord, the god and father of each individual soul, the judge of men, who passes sentence strictly according to right and wrong, rewarding goodness and punishing crime. As he reigns in the spirit world, so does Helios, the god of skies, from his sunny path watch over the doings of the living." Vol. 1, p. 226. Müller in speaking of the sacred Books of India—the Vedas says. "But hidden in this rubbish there are precious stones, only, in order to appreciate them justly, we must try to divest ourselves of the common notions of polytheism so repugnant not only to our feelings, but to our understanding. No doubt if, we must employ technical terms, the religion of the Veda is polytheism, not monotheism, deities are invoked by different names, some clear and intelligible, such as Agni, fire; Sûrya, the sun; Ushas, dawn; Maruts, the storms; Prithevî, the earth; Ap, the waters; Nadi, the rivers: others, such as Varuna, Mitra, Indra, which have become proper names, and disclose but dimly their original application to the great aspects of nature, the sky, the sun, the day. But whenever one of these individual gods is invoked, he is not conceived of as limited by the powers of others, as superior or inferior in rank. Each god is to the mind of the supplicant as good as all gods. He is felt at the time as a real divinity,—as supreme and absolute,—without a suspicion of those limitations, which, to our minds, a plurality of gods must entail on every single god." Chips from a German Workshop, Vol. I, p. 27. "Thus in one hymn, Agni (fire) is called 'the ruler of the universe,' 'the lord of men,' the wise king, the father, the brother, the son, the friend of man; nay all the powers and names of the other gods are distinctly ascribed to Agni," idem p. 28. And what more could human language achieve in trying to express the idea of a divine and supreme power, than what another poet says of another god Varunat [heaven]. "Thou art lord of all, of heaven and earth; thou art king of all, of those who are gods, and of those who are men, idem, p. 28. In "Whitney's Oriental and Linguistic studies" the character of this Varuna (heaven), which is considered to be identical with the Greek Ουρανος (heaven), is thus drawn; "He is the orderer and ruler of the universe. He established the eternal laws which govern the movements of the world, and which neither mortals nor immortals may break. He regulated the seasons. He appointed sun, moon and stars their courses. He gave to each creature that which is its peculiar characteristic. In a no less degree is he a moral governor; to the Adityas [the twelve sun-gods of which Varuna is the central figure], and to him in particular, attach themselves very remarkable, almost Christian ideas respecting moral right and wrong, transgression and its punishment, * * *. It is a sore grief to the poets that man daily transgresses Varuna's commands. They acknowledge that without his aid, they are not masters of a single moment; they fly to him for refuge from evil, expressing at the same time all confidence that their prayers will be heard and granted. From his station in the heavens, Varuna sees and hears everything; nothing can remain hidden from him," p. 43. One of the hymns to Varuna, as translated by Müller, reads thus: verse 10. "He, the upholder of order, Varuna sits down among his people; he, the wise, sits there to govern. 11, From thence perceiving all wondrous things, he sees what has been, and what will be done." 19, O hear this my calling, Varuna, be gracious now, longing for help I have called upon thee. 20, Thou, O wise god, art lord of all, of heaven and earth; listen on thy way." In another hymn. Varuna is almost spoken of as a creator, "Wise and mighty are the works of him who stemmed asunder the wide firmaments. He lifted on high the bright and glorious heaven, he stretched out apart the starry sky and the earth." And in another he is addressed as the god, who has mercy for sinners.—1, "Let me not yet, O Varuna, enter into the house of clay; have mercy, almighty, have mercy. 2, If I go along trembling, like a cloud driven by the wind; have mercy, almighty, have mercy. 5, Whenever we men, O Varuna, commit an offence before the heavenly host; whenever we break thy law through thoughtlessness: have mercy, almighty, have mercy." Again in a hymn to Varuna it is said. 3, I ask,

O Varuna, wishing to know this my sin. I go to ask the wise. The sages all tell me the same; Varuna it is, who is angry with thee. 4, Was it an old sin, O Varuna, that thou wished to destroy thy friend who always praises thee? Tell me, thou unconquerable lord, and I will quickly turn to thee with praise, freed from sin. 5, Absolve us from the sins of our father's and from those which we committed with our own bodies. 6, It was not our own doing, O Varuna, it was necessity (temptation), an intoxicating draft, passion, vice, thoughtlessness. The old is there to mislead the young; even sleep brings unrighteousness. 7, Let me without sin give satisfaction to the angry god like a slave to the bounteous lord. The lord god enlightened the foolish; he the wisest leads his worshipper to wealth. 8, O lord, Varuna, may this song go well to thy heart. May we prosper in keeping and acquiring. Protect us, O gods, always with your blessing." The consciousness of sin is a prominent feature of the religion of the Veda. So is likewise the belief that the gods are able to take away from man the heavy burden of his sins. The next hymn, which is taken from the Athava Veda (1V. 16). Will show how near the language of the ancient poets of India may approach to the language of the Bible:—"1, The great lord of these worlds sees as if he were near. If a man thinks he is walking by stealth, the gods know it all. 2, If a man stands or walks or hides, if he goes to lie down or to get up, what two people sitting together whisper, king Varuna knows it; he is there as the third. 3, This earth, too, belongs to Varuna, the king, and this wide sky with its ends far apart. The two seas (the sky and the ocean) are Varuna's loins: he is also contained in this small drop of water. 4, He who should flee far beyond the sky, even he would not be rid of Varuna. His spies proceed from heaven towards this world: with thousand eyes they overlook this earth. 5, King Varuna sees all this, what is between heaven and earth, and what is beyond. He has counted the twinklings of the eyes of men. As a player throws the dice, he settles all things." Chips from a German Workshop, Vol. I, pp, 39–42.

The character of Zeus the chief god of the Greeks, is thus given by Smith in his Classical-Dictionary, art. Zeus.--"He is called the father of gods and men, the most high and powerful among the immortals, whom all others obey. He is the supreme ruler, who with his counsel manages every thing; the founder of kingly power, and of law and of order, whence Dice, Themis and Nemesis are his assistants. For the same reason, he protects the assembly of the people, the meetings of the council, and as he presides over the whole state, so also over every house and family. He also watched over the sanctity of the oath, and the laws of hospitality, and protected suppliants. He avenged those who were wronged, and punished those who had committed a crime, for he watched the doings and sufferings of all men. He was also the original source of all prophetic power, from him all prophetic sounds and signs proceeded. Everything good as well as bad comes from Zeus; according to his own choice he assigns good or evil to mortals; and fate itself was subordinate to him," p. 830.

The character of the Greek Zeus is thus drawn by the poet Aeschylus as stated by prof. Tyler in his "Theology of the Greek Poets." The character of the supreme deity, as it is generally represented in the other tragedies, and as it appears in the epithets by which he is addressed by the chorus, corresponds much more nearly with our ideas of the true God. He is the universal father—father of gods and men; the universal cause (παναίτιος, Agamem. 1485); the all-seer and all-doer πανεόπτης, πανεργέτης Ibid. and sup. 139); the all-wise and all-controlling (παγκρατής Sup. 818); the just and the executor of justice (δἰκηφόρος, Agamem. 525); true and incapable of falsehood (Prom. 1031); holy (ἁγνός, Sup. 650), merciful (πρευμενης, Ibid. 139); the god especially of the suppliant and the stranger (supplices, passim); the most high and perfect one (τέλειον ὑψιστον, Eumen. 28; "King of kings, of the happy the most happy; of the perfect most perfect power; blessed Zeus," (Sup. 522).

The general resemblance, suggested by these attributes, between the supreme god of the Greek tragedies, and of the Hebrew Scripture, derives additional force from the frequency with which, as we shall see, he is spoken of as a jealous god, visiting the iniquities of the fathers upon the children; one who will by no means clear the guilty; whose mysterious providence is an unfathomable abyss, and before whose irresistible power the heavens and the earth are shaken, and gods and men are as nothing. Theol. of the Greek Poets, pp. 213-15.

The same authority gives the character of the Latin god Jupiter, as follows: "his name signifies the father or lord of heaven, being a contraction of Diovispater, or Diespiter. Being the lord of heaven, he was worshipped as god for rain, storms, and lightening. In consequence of his possessing such powers over the elements, and especially of his always having the thunderbolt at his command, he was regarded as the highest and most powerful among the gods. Hence he is called the best and most high (Optimus Maximus). His temple at Rome stood on the lofty hill of the Capitol, whence he derived the names of Capitolinus and Tarpeias. He was regarded as the special protector of Rome. As such he was worshipped by the Consuls on entering upon their office; and the triumph of a victorious general was a solemn procession to his temple." Art. Jupiter, p. 358.

"In Babylon and Assyria we find as supreme god. At the head of the Assyrian pantheon stood the "great god" Asshur. His usual titles are "the great lord," "the king of all the gods," "he, who rules supreme over the gods." Sometimes he is called "the father of the gods," though that is a title which is more properly assigned to Belus. His place is first in invocations. He is regarded throughout all the Assyrian inscriptions as the special tutelary deity both of the kings and the country. He places the monarchs upon their thrones, firmly establishes them in the government, lengthens the years of their reigns, preserves their power, protects their forts and arms, etc. To him they look to give them the victory over their enemies, to grant them all the wishes of their heart.

They represent themselves as passing their lives in his service. It is to spread his worship, that they carry on their wars. Unlike other gods, Asshur had no notorious temple or shrine in any particular city, a sign that his worship was spread equally throughout the whole land, and was not to any extent localized. The Assyrian religion is "the worship of Asshur." No similar phrases are used with respect to any of the other gods of the pantheon. It is indicative of the (comparatively speaking) elevated character of Assyrian polytheism, that this exalted and awful deity continued, from first to last, the main object of worship, and was not superseded in the thoughts of men by the lower and more intelligible divinities." Rawlinson's Anc. Monarchies, II. 2, 3. "In the time of the twelfth dynasty of their kings, more than two thousand years before Christ, and before the days of Abraham, the Unity of God was still not so far obscured but that each district or great city had only its one great object of worship. The union of all the districts into one kingdom constituted the primitive polytheism of Egypt. Thus Phtah was god as worshipped in Memphis; Ra, in the holy city of On; Khem in Khemmis in the Thebiad, and Amun in the city of Thebis. Phtah was regarded as the creator of the world; Khem as the father of men. Ra as the god of light, represented by the sun, and Amun, as the almighty and inscrutable power of deity. The commonest symbol of God, in all parts of Egypt, was the sun. It seems to have been conceived of as a sign of the governing power of God. The kings of Egypt always bore an image of the sun's disk upon their seal; and the name of the sun-god Ra, entered as an element into their royal title, and they were all sons of Ra." Moffat's Comparative Hist. of Religions, Vol. II. p. 77.

These quotations might be multiplied indefinitely showing that all the ancient nations of the world ascribed many of the attributes and works of the true God to the chief god of their respective countries. But this will suffice.—They also show that they had the idea of a certain kind of unity and supremacy as belonging to the deity—as also benevolence, clemency, justice and universal government. They had a deep conviction that the good would be rewarded and the wicked punished, that a revelation from God might be expected, that help might be obtained in the time of distress, and also help to live virtuously. They all had the knowledge of the external rites of religion, consisting in the offering of prayers, sacrifices, thank offerings and worship with the singing or chanting of hymns. There was a knowledge that the will of God regulated the affairs of the world, set up kings and put down princes. Indeed it is most remarkable to what an extent the knowledge of the great truths in reference to God and man, and of man's relation to and his duty to God was transmitted by tradition among all the early nations after the dispersion. "On those monuments [of Egypt] appear pictorial representations of gods, priests, worshippers in acts of sacrifice, offerings, prayer, adoration, in religious processions and the various attitudes of worship. Of the books described by Clement, as those of Hermes (Thoth), the first was one of hymns to the gods: the second contained the whole duty of a king's wife." Moffat's Comp. Hist. Rel. Vol. I. p. 61." Apparently the most ancient and highly valued of all was the book containing the hymns to the gods" Ib. p. 62. The "Book of the death" or the "Funeral Ritual" of the Egyptians is in some respects the most remarkable book which has come down from the past, and makes it clear that the ancients had a much clearer idea of the doctrine of future rewards and punishment, than has been hitherto supposed, they had.

I proceed to remark that Jehovah has some *essential* characteristics which distinguish him from all other beings. And while in some there may be a resemblance to him, yet before any being bearing another name can be considered as identically the same with him, it must be shown beyond all doubt that he has those attributes and works which are the essential characteristics of Jehovah.

One special distinguishing characteristic of Jehovah is this—he his *eternally self existent.* "The Lord said unto Moses, I am that I am; and he said, thus shalt thou say unto the children of Israel, I am hath sent me to you. "Ex. 3: 14. "Before the mountains were brought forth, or ever thou hadst formed the earth or the world, even from everlasting to everlasting, thou art God." Ps. 90: 2. "Thy throne is established of old, thou art from everlasting." Ps. 93: 2. "For thus saith the High and lofty One that inhabiteth eternity." Is. 57: 15. "The everlasting God, the Lord, the Creator of the ends of the earth, fainteth not neither is weary." Is. 40; 28. "Thy name is from everlasting." Is. 63: 16. "Art thou not from everlasting O Jehovah my God, mine Holy One?" Hab. 1: 12. "Thus saith Jehovah, I am the first and I am the last and beside me there is no God." Is. 44: 6. Such are some of the declarations of the Bible in regard to Jehovah—The late Rev. W. H. Medhurst D.D. in his "Inquiry into the proper mode of rendering the word God &c.," say: "We do not find that the Chinese predicate of him [*i. e.* Shangti] self-existence; nor do we remember any place in which they expressly describe him as existing from eternity," p. 5. Dr. Legge admits that it has not been shown that the Chinese declare Shangti to be self-existent. "This" he says, "may still be urged as a bar to the conclusion that he is the true god. Be it so, that a proposition in so many words to that effect, has not yet been produced ; yet, I contend that the natural conclusion from the passages which I have brought forward, is, that Shangti is self-existent." "Notions of the Chinese," p. 32. So it might be said, that it would be a "natural conclusion" from the statements which have been quoted above in regard to the chief god of every other nation, that he was self-existent. But in a matter of such transcendent importance, we cannot be satisfied with any "natural conclusion" or mere inference, we want some clear and positive statements before we can accept the opinion that the Chinese have considered Shangti as self-existent.

There is a second *essential* characteristic, which Jehovah declares belongs to him, and which is not ascribed to Shangti. Jehovah justly and rightfully claims for himself exclusively the religious homage and worship of all his rational creatures. He says, "I am Jehovah, thy God.** Thou shalt have no other gods before me. Thou shalt not make unto thee any graven image, or any likeness of anything that is in heaven above, or that is in the earth beneath, or that is in the water under the earth; thou shalt not bow down thyself to them, nor serve them: for I, Jehovah thy God, am a jealous God, visiting the iniquity of the fathers upon the children unto the third and fourth generation of them that hate me; and shewing mercy unto thousands of them that love me and keep my commandments Ex. 20; 2-6. That of which Jehovah is jealous is the giving of religious worship to any other being beside himself. The Bible every where declares that any form of idolatry is the object of his special displeasure, and that it will receive his most condign punishment. "For thou shalt worship no other God; for Jehovah whose name is Jealous, is a jealous God, Ex. 34: 14. "Take heed unto yourselves, lest ye forget the covenant of Jehovah your God, which he made with you, and make you a graven image, or the likeness of anything which Jehovah, thy God, hath forbidden thee; for Jehovah thy God is a consuming fire, even a jealous God." Deut. 4: 23, 24, "Ye shall not go after other gods, of the gods of the people which are round about you; (for Jehovah thy God is a jealous God among you;) lest the anger of Jehovah, thy God, be kindled against you, and destroy you from the face of the earth." Deut. 6: 14, 15. "And Joshua said unto the people, Ye cannot serve Jehovah; for he is a holy God; he is a jealous God; he will not forgive your transgressions and your sins. If ye forsake Jehovah and serve strange gods, then he will turn and do you hurt and consume you after that he hath done you good." Josh. 24; 19. 20. "For they will turn away thy son from following me, that they may serve other gods: so will the anger of Jehovah be kindled against thee, and destroy thee suddenly." Deut. 7: 4. These are a few of the many passages in which Jehovah has expressed his displeasure at every form and kind of idolatry. But nowhere do the Chinese attribute any such feelings to Shangti. So far from any such feelings being ascribed to him, in the great sacrifice which is made to heaven at the winter solstice by the emperor of China, and which sacrifice Dr. Legge says is offered to Shangti, other objects are associated with Shangti as receivers of the sacrifice. This concurrent worship of other objects in connection with Shangti has existed in China from the very earliest period of which we have any records. "The chiefs and rulers of the ancient Chinese were not without some considerable knowledge of god [i. e. Shangti]; but they were accustomed, on their first appearance in the country, if the earliest portions of the Shoo can be relied on at all, to worship other spiritual beings as well. Shun had no sooner been designated by Yaou to the active duties of the government as co-emperor with him, than he offered a special sacrifice, but with the ordinary forms of god [Shangti]; sacrificed purely to the six honoured ones; offered their appropriate sacrifices to the rivers and hills, and extended his worship to the hosts of spirits." [i. e. Shin] Legge's Shoo-king. Prolegomena, p. 192, 193. The

Chinese have no idea that such feelings, as those which Jehovah expresses as belonging to himself in regard to the worship of any other being or object, pertain to Shangti, or any of the gods. Many of this people on reading the 2nd, Commandment, have expressed surprise that Jehovah is represented as having this characteristic, as they consider such feelings as derogatory to the divine character. Here then is a second essential characteristic of Jehovah which does not belong to Shangti.

In the third place I remark, that the Bible everywhere presents as the great and distinguishing work of Jehovah, that he is the creator of the heavens, the earth, the sea and all things which are in them. "For in six days, Jehovah made heaven and earth, the sea, and all that in them is." Ex. 20: 11. Jehovah hath made the earth by his power, he hath established the world by his wisdom and he hath stretched out the heavens by his discretion. Jer. 10: 12. "In the beginning God created the heavens and the earth." Gen. 1: 1. "Thou even thou art Jehovah alone. Thou hast made heaven, and the heaven of heavens, with all their hosts, the earth and all things that are therein, the seas and all that is therein, and thou preservest them all; and the host of heaven worshippeth thee." Neh. 9: 6. "Thus saith Jehovah, I have made the earth, and created man upon it; I, even my hands, have stretched out the heavens, and all their hosts have I commanded." Is. 45: 12. "I am Jehovah, that maketh all things; that stretcheth forth the heavens alone; that spreadeth abroad the earth by myself." Is. 44: 24. "Thou art worthy, O Lord, to receive glory, and honor, and power, for thou hast created all things and for thy pleasure they are and were created." Rev. 4: 11. These are a few of the almost innumerable passages in the Bible, which refer to Jehovah as the creator of the heavens and the earth. They are however sufficient to show the prominence which is given in the S. S. to this great work of Jehovah. But how different is it in all Chinese literature. The Rev. Dr. Medhurst says, "In one important particular, the Chinese ideas, respecting God fall short of the truth, for they do not appear to ascribe the creation of heaven and earth to any one being." An Inquiry, &c. p. 4. Moffat in his Comp. Hist. of Rel. says. "In the historical classics of China, there is no mention of creation, nor of anything prior to the reign of King Yaou. Later traditions on the subject, as they do not belong to Chinese scripture, do not come under this head. The cosmological theories of mythologers and philosophers have no right to be assigned to the credit of the original national faith." Vol. II, p. 7. He also remarks that "creation out of nothing does not appear in the religion of Greece." Ibid. p. 12. This all agrees with the general remark that the creation of all things out of nothing is not spoken of in any heathen system. Whatever semblance of creation that may be spoken of in heathen writers refers to the transformation of pre-existing matter. I am fully aware that Dr. Legge maintains that the work of creation is ascribed to Shangti. But as Moffat has stated, there is no reference to the creation of heaven and earth out of nothing in the Shoo-King as translated by Dr. L. The strongest passage which he brings forward in support of his opinion is a hymn in praise of Shangti, which was prepared in the 17th year of the emperor Kea-tsing, about the year 1539, A.D. and which is found in "The Collected Statutes of Ming Dynasty." But if we could admit Dr. Legge's translation as correct, it can hardly be claimed that a hymn of the date of 1539, A.D. is an expression of the opinions of the people who lived 1000 or 1500 years before Christ. There were several sources from which the Chinese scholars of A.D. 1539 might have obtained some idea of the Bible account of the creation. The Jews came to China, if not before, very soon after the Christian era. The Nestorians came in the year A.D. 505 and were here for more than three hundred years. The Mohammedans came in the 8th century and the Roman Catholics at the end of the 13th century. See Williams' Middle King. Vol. II, pp. 290-99. But apart from this, the accuracy of the translation is not admitted. One word which he translates *creation*, is held by many not to have that meaning—and among others who hold this opinion, is the Rev. Dr. Medhurst. To his learing in Chinese Dr. Legge has given strong testimony. In his preface to the Shoo-King he says: "Dr. Medhurst's attainments in Chinese were prodigious." p. vi. He also dedicates one of his pamphlets to the Rev. Dr. Medhurst "in token of his admiration of the extent and depth of his acquaintance with the Chinese language and literature." In "a Dissertation on the Theology of the Chinese." Dr. M. says: "The words Tsaou hwa, here translated 'production and change,' are not to be rendered 'creation and transformation;' for the Chinese have *no idea of creation*, as we understand it; viz. *the bringing the world into existence*. It is true, the writer above quoted, explains production by the bringing of something out of nothing; but by that the Chinese mean, the birth of animals, the springing up of plants, the advancing of the tides, or the blowing of the wind, when to all appearance, nothing was before. They do *not mean by it, the original formation of all things*, but the constant production of things observable every day." p. 16. As the Chinese in common with all other heathen nations had not the conception of the creation of heaven and earth and all things out of nothing it is self evident that they could not ascribe such a work to Shangti. From all these testimonies and considerations, it appears clear that the Chinese *have not ascribed* the great and characteristic work of Jehovah to Shangti.

From the above course of reasoning, it is evident that Shangti is without two of the most essential characteristic attributes that belong to Jehovah, viz., eternal self-existence and that holy jealousy which requires the religious service of all his creatures to himself. Neither has he had the most distinguishing work of Jehovah ascribed to him. In the celebrated case already referred to, the claimant to the Tichbourne estates had an outward resemblance to the true heir, he had acquired a considerable knowledge of the mental habits, acquirements and acquaintances of the heir, so as to present a strong presumption in the minds of many that he was the identical person. But when it was found that he was destitute of those things which most *distinctively* belonged to the heir, such as, the knowledge of the members of the heir's own family—the ability to speak and read French which he had known like his own tongue,—the knowledge of the places and studies of the college where he studied, &c., all candid and considerate persons concurred with the learned judge and the jury in the opinion that the claimant *was not the same* person as the true heir. So notwithstanding that Dr. Legge, in the earnest advocacy of Shangti was so hopeful as to express his belief in these words.—" I am confident the Christian world will agree with me in saying, this god [Shangti] is our God"—I feel assured that the great body of Christian men will agree in the conclusion—that, while the Chinese have ascribed to Shangti many of the attributes and works which belong to Jehovah, just as many others of the ancient nations did to their supreme god, yet Shangti is not the same being as Jehovah,—who alone is "God over all blessed for ever." Any one of these three lines of argument, viz. 1st, The testimony of the sacred Scriptures that all nations have forgotten the true God. 2nd, The evidence furnished by various writers that in the early ages of the world all nations ascribed many of the attributes and works of Jehovah to their respective chief gods and hence that such ascription is not any proof that any one of them is Jehovah. 3rd, The evidence that Shangti is without some of the most characteristic and essential attributes and works of Jehovah—would be sufficient to satisfy most minds, that the opinion that Shangti is the same being as Jehovah *is not tenable;* but when they all converge to the same point, they establish the negative of the proposition and prove beyond all reasonable doubt that Shangti *is not* the same being as Jehovah. They will also serve yet more to establish all minds in the truth which has been held by the worshippers of Jehovah in all ages, that *all the nations* had departed from the one true God, and made to themselves false gods and make evident the interpretation that *"all the gods* of the nations are idols but Jehovah made the heavens." Ps. 96 : 5.

Whilst therefore, it would be a great vantage ground in prosecuting missionary labour in China, if it were true that Shangti of the classics is the same being as Jehovah, yet as it is not true, we must not compromise the truth for any supposed advantage. And however distasteful it may be to the pride of the Chinese, especially to the literary classes, to declare to them that the Shangti of the classics, as well as Yuh hwang Shangti, is a false god, and that no worship of him can be acceptable to Jehovah, yet we must in faithfulness to our God declare the whole truth to them; and exhort them to turn from the worship of Shangti and all other false gods to the worship of Jehovah, the only living and true God and from whom alone cometh salvation.

PART II,

What Being is Designated Shang-Ti in the Chinese Classics and in the Ritual of the State Religion of China.

I MIGHT end this discussion with the close of Part first. But it appears to me very desirable that some satisfactory answer should be given to the question which is often asked, viz., who or what is Shangti of the Chinese Classics? It is most natural to suppose that the Chinese books give some definite information on a matter of such importance. Having arrived, after months of careful study and pains-taking inquiry, at a definite conclusion in my own mind, I proceed to place the matter before my readers with the reasons which have led me to these results. It is my sincere conviction that the evidence which is submitted to them for consideration will satisfy most readers that the conclusion, at which I have arrived, is well founded.

In order to give a satisfactory view of the matter, it will be necessary to take some notice of the religions of China. It is generally represented that there are three systems of religion prevailing in China, which are commonly styled, Confucianism, Taouism and Buddhism. Buddhism, as is well known, was introduced into China from India, in the first century of the Christian era. Taouism originated from the teachings of Laoutsz, who was contemporaneous with Confucius. With these two systems of religion, my inquiries, at this time, have nothing to do. Their origin was entirely subsequent to that of Confucianism; and whilst it might be interesting to consider the causes which have resulted in these two systems superseding, to such an extent, the primitive worship of China, I refrain from entering upon such an interesting subject and restrict my inquiries entirely to the consideration of Confucianism. Here also I must pursue further this course of elimination; for Confucianism, as commonly spoken of, comprehends two distinct systems, viz., a system of ethical and political doctrines, and a system of religious worship. The former of these has attracted the principal attention of the students of Chinese history, and the latter has been in a great measure overlooked. At this present time I confine my inquiries to this latter subject, the early system of religious worship which prevailed among the Chinese, before the introduction of Taouism and Buddhism.

We have no clear statement of the time of the commencement of this primitive worship. We may, however, suppose that it commenced very soon after the settlement of this branch of the human race in China—or, in a general way, we may say that it commenced more than two thousand years before the Christian era. This early worship was the only kind that was known to Confucius: and all the terms used in connection with religion and the remarks made by him in relation thereto, refer to this system. This fact should be carefully kept in mind in reference to the different Chinese authors who have written in regard to it; for a great many of the different opinions and statements which have been published in the discussion of these matters have come from want of a proper discrimination of the time when the different Chinese authors lived and wrote.

This worship, which had its origin in the earliest ages of the Chinese race, is of that same simple character which has been found to have prevailed among the nations of central and western Asia and eastern Europe. Men not liking to retain the knowledge of Jehovah in their minds, and looking at the external objects, from which the blessings of rain and sunshine, fruitful seasons and the abundant supply of the grains and fruits of the earth were received, gave the worship and service, which was due to the Creator alone, to these external objects. They worshipped the heaven's, the sun, the moon and the stars, and all the elements, as the wind, the clouds, the rain and the thunder; the earth and all its component parts, as the five mountains and the five hills, the four seas and the four rivers.

Though this primitive worship has been so much overshadowed by Taouism and Buddhism in the outward appearances, by the number of their temples and services, their priests and their ceremonies, yet its influence is felt in all the religious sentiments of the Chinese people; and this worship is much practiced, though it does not attract much attention, amidst the more imposing ceremonies of the other systems. Thus the worship of heaven and earth is a part of the worship performed in connection with marriage ceremonies and also at funerals, in some parts of China. The worship of the local earth-god in every house every morning and evening, is a part of this early worship, as is also the observance of the new and full moon as days of special worship—the worship of the moon in the eighth month and many others ceremonies which will be referred to hereafter.

Of the primitive worship in other lands, Moffat in his "Comparative History of Religions," says "In the oriental world the greatest of the gods were, throughout the whole of what we have defined as the ancient period, taken from the great objects of nature; but latterly disguised by combination with meaner things," Vol. II, p. 62. "In the history of the Greek religion there are several stages. The earliest on record was a pure nature worship, in which the divine beings were all symbolical of things in nature. Such also were Heaven, Earth, Aether, Day, Sky, Mountains, Sea, Ocean, Sun, Moon, Aurora, streams, woods, seasons and various products of the soil. In that stage the mythology of Greece was of the same class with that of the Hindu in the Rig.—Veda. It's gods were the same, and some of the names were identical." Ibid. p. 65. Smith's Dict. of the Bible in the Article on Idolatry, says, "The old religion of the Shemitic races consisted, in the opinion of Movers, in the deification of the powers and laws of nature. * * The sun and moon were early selected as the outword symbols of this all prevailing power, and the worship of the heavenly bodies was not only the most ancient, but the most prevalent system of idolatry. Taking its rise in the plains of Chaldea, it spread through Egypt, Greece Scythia and even Mexico and Ceylon." English Abbreviated Ed. p. 342. With these statements as regards the early worship of the nations of Western Asia and Eastern Europe, the statement of the early worship of the Chinese as given by Dr. Legge, mainly agrees. "Shun had no sooner been designated by Yaou to the active duties of the government as co-emperor with him, than 'he offered a special sacrifice, but with the ordinary forms, to God [the word in the original is *Shang-ti*]; sacrificed purely to the six honored ones; offered their appropriate sacrifices to the rivers and hills; and extended his worship to the hosts of the spirit's [Shin]. Subsequently, in the progresses which he is reported to have made to the different mountains, where he met the princes of the several quarters of the empire, he always commenced his proceedings with them by 'presenting a burnt offering to heaven, and sacrificing in order to the hills and rivers.'" (This offering was made B.C. 2283). "Who the six honored ones" whom Shun sacrificed to, next to God, [Shang-ti] were, is not known—(according to the Chinese Commentators they were "the seasons, cold and heat, sun, moon, stars, and drought.") In going to worship the hills and rivers, and the hosts of the spirits, he must have supposed that there were certain tutelary beings who presided over the more conspicuous objects of nature, and its processes." Shoo King, Prolog. p. 92. Again in Shi King, Dr. Legge says "While the ancient Chinese thus believed in God [Shang-ti], and thus conceived of him, they believed in other spirits [Shin] under him, some presiding over hills and rivers, and others dwelling in the heavenly bodies. In fact there was no object to which a tutelary spirit [or god] might not at times be ascribed." Prolog. p. 132. The early worship of the Japanese appears to have been very nearly the same as that of the Chinese. It is thus represented by the late Bishop Smith, in his "Ten weeks in Japan." "Hence it has come to pass that the Sinto religion is in a peculiar manner 'the way of the Kami,' and abounds with shrines erected to the popular divinities of the earth and water, the sea, the sky and the mountains, peopling every nook and corner with the objects of idolatrous worship, and teaching the common people to find a god in every place. The great "Sun—goddess" at the present time seems, to be the principal object of divine adoration to the multitude, pp. 45, 46. In this last particular, the Japanese agree with the Egyptians and Syrians in making the sun the chief object of worship, and in this differed from the Chinese, who made heaven and earth the principal objects of their worship.

In China from the earliest periods, the worship of ancestors has also prevailed in connection with this general worship of the objects of nature. In relation to this, Dr. Legge says, "There was also among the early Chinese the religious worship of their departed friends, which still continues to be observed by all classes from the emperor downward, and seems of all religious services to have the greatest hold upon the people. The rule of Confucius, that 'parents when dead, should be sacrificed to according to propriety,' was, doubtless, in accordance with a practice which had come down from the earliest times of the nation." Shoo King Prolog. p. 194.

We have thus arrived at the result that the objects of nature and their ancestors, were the objects of worship among the Chinese people from the earliest period of their history.

In the Chinese handbook which is called the "Three Character Classic," the objects of their worship are very summarily referred to in the line, "There are three powers, heaven, earth and man." In the fuller statement of the matter these are more fully expressed as "天神 Tien-shin, 地祇 Ti-k'i and 人鬼 jin-kwei." The "Tien-shin" not only refers to deified heaven specifically, but it is used to refer to all the component parts thereof as the sun, the moon and stars, and the elements wind, rain, clouds and thunder; so also the Tiki not only refers to deified earth specifically, but, also it is used in refering to the various parts of the earth as the five mountains, the five hills, the four seas and the four rivers, and the jin-kwei not only includes the *manes* of deceased parents, but it includes the *manes* of public benefactors, who for their supposed merit have been deified; such as those who are called the "gods of the land and of the grains,"—"the god agriculture" and the goddess of silk culture." These are the gods which an agricultural people, as the Chinese are, would soon make to themselves. Dr. Legge, in a note on the passage of the Shoo King. "Heaven and earth is the parent of all creatures," says, "there can be no doubt that the deification of 'heaven and earth,' which appears in the text, took its rise from the Yih King, of which King Wăn may properly be regarded as the author. No one who reads what Wăn says on the first and second diagrams, and the further explanation of his son Tan (Duke of Chow) can be surprised to find King Woo speaking as he does in the text." Shoo King, vol. ii, p. 283.

These objects were not only the objects of worship among the people, but also were worshipped by the kings and rulers of the people. The worship of "heaven and earth" more especially pertained to the chief ruler of the kingdom. And notwithstanding the extent to which the ceremonies of Taouism and Buddhism have superseded those of the primitive worship among the people, this early religion of the country consisting in the worship of the objects of nature and of ancestors continues to be the *State religion* of this empire. We have in this, the singular fact, that the same system of religion has continued to be the recognized state religion of this people for the long period of more than four thousand years. And as this is the oldest state religion, it is also the most imposing in its ceremonies of any other system of false religion, except perhaps the worship of Jupiter on the Capitoline Hill in Imperial Rome on special occasions, as when a triumphant general went in grand procession to the temple of Jupiter to return thanks for victory. In the Imperial city of Peking, there are nearly twenty altars and temples connected with this state religion. Some of them are the most imposing structures in the city. Some of these altars and buildings are as follows; the altar to Heaven with the adjoining blue dome made to represent the vault of Heaven and other buildings connected with the worship at that altar on the south of the city. The altar to earth out of the north-gate. The temple to the Imperial ancestors to the east of the altar to Heaven, and the Temple to the gods of the land and of the grain near to that of the ancestors. The altar to the god of agriculture to the west of the altar of Heaven. The altar to the Sun on the east of the city, and of the Moon on the west of the city. The temple to Confucius, to the Sages of all ages, to the kings of previous dynasties, to the god of the year, &c., &c. Instead of giving my own statement of the sacrifices which are offered to the various objects and persons, I prefer to copy the account of the State religion of China as given by the distinguished scholar and missionary the late Rev. R. Morrison, D.D., on the last year of his life in the "Chinese Repository" for 1834 at page 49. The statement, he tells his readers, was compiled from "The collected Statutes" of this Dynasty and from collected "Laws" of the empire. "The collected Statutes" of this Dynasty "has been published in at least two editions; one was published in the 29th year of Kien-lung and the other in the 24th year of Kia-king or in the year, A. D. 1765 and 1819.

The latter edition is bound in 240 vols. and the account of the rites and ceremonies at these sacrifices with the prayers that are offered, and the hymns that are sung fill some 30 vols. of the work. Dr. Morrison writes; "The State religion as practised by the Court of Peking and the Provincial governments, is contained in the collected statutes" and "Code of Laws" of this dynasty under the head of "rites and ceremonies," and in the subordinate head of 'sacrifices and offerings.' From these two works, we shall briefly specify the persons or things to whom these sacrifices are presented or the objects of governmental worship. These are chiefly things, although persons are also included. The state sacrifices are divided into three classes; first, the great sacrifices; second, the medium sacrifices; and third, the little sacrifices. In the following list, the 1st, 2nd, 3rd, and 4th, are the objects, or the classes of objects, to which the great sacrifices are offered; [These four are Heaven, Earth, the Imperial ancestors and the gods of the land and the grain]. From the 5th, to the 13th, are those to which the medium sacrifices are offered; that of the 14th and onward have right only to the little sacrifices.

1. T'ien, the Heavens or sky. This object of worship is otherwise called the azure heavens; and hwang kung yü "the imperial concave expanse.

2. Ti, the Earth. This, like the heavens, is dignified with the epithet imperial.

3. Tae Meaou, 'The great temple' of Ancestors. This title is used, to include all the tablets contained therein dedicated to the manes, or shades of the deceased emperors of the present dynasty. This triad of titles, the Heavens, the Earth, the great temple, always placed together on a level in respect of dignity at the great sacrifices, are also worshipped apart.

4. Shay tseih, the gods of the land and grain: these are the special patrons of each existing dynasty and are generally located in the fourth place. 5. The sun also called "the great light." 6. The moon, called also "the night light." 7. The manes of the emperors and kings of former ages. 8. The ancient master Confucius. 9. The ancient Patron of agriculture. 10. The ancient Patron of the manufacture of silk. 11. T'ien shin, the gods of heaven. 12. Tè ke, the gods of the earth. 13. Tae suy, the god of the passing year. [These objects from 5 to 13 inclusive receive the medium sacrifices]. 14. Seon e, the ancient patron of the healing art; together with the innumerable ghosts of deceased philanthropists, faithful statesmen, eminent scholars, martyrs to virtue, &c. 15. Sing shin, the stars. 16. The clouds. 17. The rain. 18. The wind. 19. The thunder. 20. The five great mountains of China. 21. The four seas. 22. The four rivers. 23. The famous hills. 24. The great streams of water. 25. Military flags and banners. 26. The god of the road, where an army may pass. 27. The god of cannon. 28. The gods of the gate. 29. The queen goddess of the ground. 30. The north pole, &c., &c." From this specimen it is apparent that in the Chinese State religion, the material universe, as a whole and in detail, is worshipped; and that subordinate thereto, they have gods celestial and terrestrial and ghosts infernal; that they worship the work of their own hands, not only as images of persons or things divine, but human workmanship for earthly purposes, as in flags and banners and destructive cannon. That the *material universe* is the object of worship appears not only from the names of those several parts which have been given above, but also from other circumstances. Thus the imperial high-priest when he worships heaven, wears robes of azure color, in allusion to the sky. When he worships the earth, his robes are yellow to represent the clay of this earthly clod. When the sun is the object, his dress is red; and for the moon, he wears a pale white. The altar on which to sacrifice to heaven is round to represent heaven: this is expressly said." Chi. Repos. Vol. III, p. 49-51. Dr. Williams in his Middle Kingdom accepted this statement of the nature-worship of the Chinese as the correct representation of the State religion of China, Vol. II, pp. 233-234. As we close the perusal of this clear statement of the objects of the state worship by the government of this heathen people, every one must feel that he is in the presence of a wonderful system of idolatry which is an integral part of a well established government. It is calculated to impress every one with the idea of how deeply

the roots of idolatry run in the structure of this government, and how Herculean is the work of its uprooting. It is no less a work than that which was before the early disciples of our Lord, when they went forth to preach the Gospel in the Roman empire. With a view to *deepen* this impression I present the Chinese text of the sacrifices as offered by the emperor of China to Heaven and Earth, the one at the winter solstice, and the other at the summer solstice, with a translation. They are extracted from the imperial edition of the collected statutes of this dynasty as published in the 29th year of the reign of Kien-lung in the 37th and 38th sections, or Kiuen, under the part relating to the "Board of Rites and Ceremonies." The Chinese is copied as it stands on the original to show the place of honor which is assigned by the imperial authority to the different objects and persons.

TRANSLATION OF THE CHINESE RITUAL FOR THE SACRIFICE TO HEAVEN, "THE IMPERIALLY AUTHORIZED EDITION OF THE COLLECTED STATUTES OF THE GREAT PURE DYNASTY. SECTION 37TH."

Board of Rites. Bureau of Sacrifices. Great Sacrifice No. 1. All the rites of the Imperial sacrifice to Heaven must take in the South Common, where, because it is the place of the male principle (Yang), there shall be erected an altar, round in shape to resemble Heaven, which shall be called the Round Hillock. It shall consist of three terraces. Here yearly, on the day of the winter solstice, is to be offered the sacrifice to Imperial Heaven, Ruler above; to this sacrifice, as equal sharers, are to be invited Emperor T'ai Tsu Kao (T'ien Ming, 1616), Emperor T'ai Tsung Wên (T'ien Tsung, 1627), Emperor Shih Tsu Chang (Shun Chih, 1644), Emperor Sheng Tsu Jên (Kang Hi, 1662) and Emperor Shih Tsung Hien (Yung Ching, 1723); and as secondary participators the Great Light, the Night Light, the Stars, the Clouds, Rain, Wind and Thunder. The place of the Ruler above shall be in the first (topmost) terrace facing the South, that of the respective Holy Ones facing East and West. The positions of the four classes of secondary participators shall be in the second terrace; the Great Light facing West, with the Stars next to him; the Night Light facing East, with the Clouds, Rain, Wind and Thunder next to her. All these shall be covered with light blue tents. Before the Ruler Above belong an Azure gem, (an ancient jade badge of office, round with a hole in the middle) 12 bundles of silk burnt in sacrifices, 1 calf, 1 platter, 2 hampers (square outside and round within) 2 hampers (round outside and square within), flat baskets and trenchers 12 of each, 1 wine vessel, 3 cyathi, 1 furnace, 6 candlesticks and 1 roasted bullock. Before the respective Holy Ones belong equally; 1 sacrificial bundle of silk, 1 calf, 1 platter, of the two kinds of hampers two of each, flat baskets and trenchers 12 of each, 1 wine vessel, 3 cyathi, 1 furnace and 4 candlesticks. Before the Great Light and Night Light belong respectively; 1 sacrificial bundle of silk, 1 bullock, 1 platter, the two kinds of hampers 2 of each, flat baskets and trenchers 10 of each, 2 wine vessels, 3 cyathi, 20 wine cups, 1 furnace and 2 candlesticks. Before the Stars belong 11 sacrificial bundles of silk, before the Clouds, Rain, Wind, and Thunder belong 4 sacrificial bundles of silk then to these two classes respectively belong; 1 bullock; 1 sheep, 1 pig, 1 platter, 2 sacrificial broth jars, the two kinds of hampers 2 of each, flat baskets and trenchers 10 of each, 1 wine vessel, 3 cyathi; 20 wine cups, 1 furnace and 2 candlesticks. The Imperial sacrificial bundles of silk shall be placed in baskets, the sacrificial animals in trays, the wine vessels shall be full of wine and coarse cloths shall cover the spoons. The day previous to the sacrifice the Board of music shall place in readiness the musical instruments for playing the harmonious airs of Shun under the altar hanging them on the right and left. The Imperial Guard shall arrange the state traveling equipage outside of the Palace, and place the Imperial chariot at the foot of the steps of the Great Peace gate. At 9 o'clock A. M. an officer of the sacrificial Court shall go to the T'ien Ts'ing (Heavenly Pure) gate, and memorialize the Emperor to go to the Hall of Fasting. The Emperor shall then put on his Imperial dragon embroidered robes, ascend the ceremonial chair, and depart from the Palace proceeded by ten great household Lords, and followed by a retinue of two great household Lords and two companies of the Imperial Guard, twenty men in each, called the Leopard-tail bands, one of which is armed with guns and swords, the other with bows and arrows. The side escorts shall be along as usual. When the bottom of the steps of the Great Peace gate is reached, the Emperor shall leave the chair and mount the Imperial chariot. When the procession starts, all persons are to be warned off the road. The bell of the Palace shall then be rung, and while the grand Imperial equipage is moving off, those members of the royal family and all those civil and military officials who are not going to assist in the sacrifice, dressed in official robes shall all kneel to see it start. The musicians of the procession shall be there, but shall not play, one of the orderlies of the Imperial Guard, however, shall ring the bell of the Hall of Fasting. When the Emperor has entered the West gate of the altar, and arrived at the outside of the Ch'āu Hāng gate, he shall dismount from his chariot, when two ushers of the sacrificial Court, shall reverently lead the Emperor through the left door within, unto the Circular Hall of the Imperial Expanse, when before the Ruler Above and the respective Holy Ones, he shall offer incense and thereafter kneel three times and worship (kow tow) nine times. Before the shrines of the Secondary Participators in the two side vestibules, shall deputized sacrificial officers be sent to offer incense and perform the rites. Then the Emperor shall go to the Round Hillock, and look at the tablet places of the altar; then go to the treasury of the gods, and look at the baskets and trenchers and the stables of the sacrificial animals, when done he shall, by the left south gate of the inner enclosure, and through the left south gate of the outer enclosure go to the right side of the road of the gods, when he shall ascend the

Imperial chariot, and proceed to the Hall of Fasting. Those members of the royal family and those numerous officials, who are to assist in the sacrifice, dressed in their official robes shall all assemble outside of the Hall of Fasting, and there divided into companies reverently watch the Emperor enter and then retire. The rising of the sun must be watched, and when it is one hour and three quarters before sunrise, an officer of the Sacrificial Court, shall enter the Hall of Fasting to tell the time. The Emperor shall then put on his Imperial sacrificial robes, and having entered his ceremonial chair go out, then leaving his chair, he shall mount his chariot, while an orderly of the Imperial Guards rings the bell of the Hall of Fasting. When the Emperor has arrived at the outside of the south gate of the outer enclosure, at the right side of the road of the gods, he shall dismount from his chariot, whence two ushers of the Sacrificial Court shall reverently lead him within the great waiting place. The head of the Board of Rites shall then direct some officers of the Sacrificial Court to enter the Circular Hall of the Imperial Expanse, and reverently invite the tablets of the gods out; having placed them within the light blue tents, the officer of the Sacrificial Court shall then memorialize the Emperor to perform the rites. The Emperor shall then leave the great waiting place, and wash, after which the ushers of the Sacrificial Court shall reverently lead the Emperor out through the left south gate of the outer enclosure, in through the left south gate of the inner enclosure, up the main steps to the second terrace yellow tent waiting place, where he shall stand before the worshipping place there. A master of ceremonies of the Sacrificial Court, shall then lead in the four delegated sacrificial officers, entering by the right south gate to the raised middle walk at the front of the steps, when they shall stand. Officers of the Court of Ceremonies shall then lead in the relations of the Emperor and the Barons, who are to assist in the sacrifice, to their positions at the top of the steps on the third terrace; some other nobles to their positions at the bottom of the steps, and the numerous mandarins to their positions at the outside of the outer enclosure gate, where they shall stand on the right and left, facing North. The ceremonial officer shall then call the musicians and acrobats to sing a song, and the different attendants to attend to their respective duties. (Hereafter from the burning of the whole burnt offering until the taking away of the dishes and the watching of the burning, it pertains to the duty of the ceremonial officer to issue the necessary calls). The eight bands of military performers shall now enter, while the ushers shall memorialize the Emperor to take his position. The Emperor shall then take his worshipping place and stand, while the whole burnt offering is being burnt to receive the Ruler god. The incense officials, each bearing a censer, shall then enter, while the Drum Major shall command the band to play the tune for receiving the Ruler god, viz., the air of Original Peace. (All calls for music, from this time on, must be given through the musical director). Then the Master of Ceremonies shall cry "ascend the altar," whereupon they shall reverently lead the Emperor to the first terrace before the shrine of the Ruler Above. The incense officials shall then kneel and hold out the incense, the Master of Ceremonies shall then cry "kneel," the Emperor shall then kneel, cry, "offer incense," the Emperor shall then offer a stick of incense, "a second time," "a third time offering sliced sandlewood," "arise." After this he shall approach the shrines of the respective Holy Associates, and before them offer incense, the rites of which shall be the same. Then the Master of Ceremonies shall cry "return to your place;" the Emperor shall then return to his place: the Master of Ceremonies shall cry "kneel," "worship," "arise." (All the formalities of ascending the altar, and returning to the original position, and the carrying out of other ceremonies must be under the direction of a crier now and hereafter). The Emperor shall then kneel three times, and worship (kow tow) nine times, the different royal relatives and numerous officials shall all likewise follow him in these rites. The mandarins in charge of the Imperial sacrificial bundles of silk, each carrying a basket, shall now enter, while the band plays the Brilliant Peace air. Then the Emperor shall ascend the altar, and approach before the shrine of the Ruler Above. The mandarin in charge of the Imperial sacrificial bundles of silk, shall then kneel and hold out the basket, the Emperor is then to kneel, take the basket, offer the Imperial sacrificial bundles of silk, arise, and afterwards approach the shrines of the respective Associated Holy Ones, and before them offer the Imperial sacrificial bundles of silk with the same rites. The Emperor shall then return to his position, and the bowls are to be brought in. The Emperor shall then turn and stand at the side of his worshipping position, facing the West, while the proper officers shall pour the broth into jugs, and then reverently carry them from the bottom of the altar, straight up the main steps to the shrine of the Ruler Above, and the shrine of the respective Holy Ones, where they shall kneel and hold them up, then arise, and pour some of the broth into the bowls three times, after which they shall all retire descending by the west stair case. Then the Emperor shall resume his position, and while the band plays the General Peace air, the Emperor is to mount the altar, and go before the shrine of the Ruler Above, and before the shrine of the Associated Ones, where he shall kneel, offer the bowls, arise, and then return to his place The first of the (drink) offering ceremonies shall now take place. The cyathi bearers, each carrying a cyathus shall then enter. The Longevity Peace air shall be played, and the martial performance with shields and battle axes shall then be gone through with. The Emperor shall ascend the altar, and go before the shrine of the Ruler Above. The cyathi bearers shall kneel and present their cyathi, the Emperor shall likewise kneel, offer the cyathi, pour libations in the middle, arise, go to the worshipping position, which shall be his during the reading of the ritual, and stand there. The ritual officer shall then approach the ritual table, kneel, kow tow three time take up the ritual tablet, and kneel at the left of the table. The music shall now cease for a while. The Emperor shall then kneel, and likewise the whole company of mandarins. When the ritual officer shall have finished reading the ritual, he shall take the ritual tablet, approach before the shrine of the Ruler Above, kneel, place it upon the table, kow-tow three times and retire, where upon the music shall begin again. The Emperor shall now lead all his officers in worshipping three times. When he has arisen, he shall go before the shrines of the Associated Ones, and offer the cyathi successively with the same rites. The Master of Ceremonies shall then lead the delegated sacrificial officer to ascend the altar, by the east and west steps to the positions of the secondary Participators, to offer incense, to present sacrificial bundles of silk and to successively offer the cyathi; when accomplished, they shall descend and retire to their original positions. The music shall again cease. The military performers shall now retire, while the eight bands of civil performers shall enter. The Second of the (drink) offerings ceremonies shall now be carried out, during the playing of the Excellent Peace air and during the performances with feathers and fifes. The Emperor shall ascend the altar, offer successively the cyathi, pour libations on the left with the same rites as those of the First (drink) offering, and return to his place. Then shall take place the final (drink) offering during the playing of the Everlasting Peace air (the mummer's play to be the same as that of the second (drink) offering). The Emperor shall ascend the altar, offer successively the cyathi, pour libations to the right with the same rites as those of the second (drink) offering, and then return to his place. The delegated sacrificial officers shall then offer the cyathi just as on the previous occasion. The music shall cease now, while the civil mummers retire. The officer of the Sacrificial Court shall then cry "the bestowed happiness (wine) and roast meats." Two chief Butlers shall then approach the east table, take up the happiness (wine) and roast meats, enter before the shrine of the Ruler Above, and hold them up. The Emperor shall then approach the drinking-their-happiness and getting-their-flesh worshipping position, and there stand. Two members of the Imperial Guard shall then enter and stand on the left. The officers in charge of the happiness (wine) and roast meats shall then descend and stand on the right. The Emperor is then to kneel, the right and left officers on duty shall all also kneel, whereupon the right hand officers shall present the happiness wine, the Emperor shall receive the cyathus, raise it up, and pass it to the left hand officer. The roast meats shall be presented and received in the same manner. He then shall worship three times, arise, return to his place, and then lead all his officials in kneeling three times and worshipping (kow-towing) nine times. The dishes shall now be removed, while the band shall play the Glorious Peace air. An officer, whose duty it is, shall now approach before the shrine of the Ruler Above, and take away the azure gem and retire. The Ruler god shall then be dismissed to the tune of Pure Peace, while the Emperor shall lead the whole band of his officers in kneeling three times, and worshipping (kow-towing) nine times. Officers in charge shall then remove successively the ritual tablet, the sacrificial bundles of silk, the dishes, and the incense, and reverently take them to the burning place. The Emperor shall then change his position standing at the side of his worshipping place facing West, to watch the ritual and sacrificial bundles of silk pass, after which he shall resume his position. The incense and sacrificial bundles of silk belonging to the Secondary Participators, shall, likewise, by the east and west staircases, be carried to their respective burning furnaces during the performance of the Great Peace air. When the ritual and sacrificial bundles of silk shall be half burnt, the Emperor shall be memorialized to watch the burning, whereupon he shall be reverently lead through the left south gate of the inner enclosure outside to the place for watching the burning, there to witness the burning. The delegated sacrificial officers shall respectively also be led to the outside of the right hand and left hand gates to watch the burning. It shall there be memorialized to the Emperor, that the rites are over, whereupon he shall be reverently led out through the left south gate of the outer enclosure, to the great waiting place, where he shall change his clothes. Then the highest officer of the Board of Rites, shall instruct an officer of the Sacrificail Court, to reverently invite the tablet of the gods to return to the Circular Hall of the Imperial Expanse. When the Emperor shall have reached the outside of the Chau Hâng gate, he shall ascend the ceremonial chair. As the Imperial equipage proceeds, the musicians in the procession, shall play the Protecting Peace air. When the Emperor returns home, he must be followed by his relatives, but the different mandarins may successively disperse. Those relatives and numerous officials, who did not assist at the sacrifice, shall be dressed in their official robes to kneel and receive the Emperor outside of the Palace. While the bell of the Palace is ringing, the different relations shall follow the Imperial chariot within, unto the inner gold water bridge, where they shall reverently watch the Emperor enter the Palace, and then one and all disperse."

THE RITUAL FOR PRAYER TO HEAVEN ON ANY SPECIAL OCCASION.

If for any reason a prayer should be reverently offered, a delegated officer shall take charge of the service. At the fifth watch, the Sacrificial Court shall see that the light blue tents are put up on the Round Hillock. At the first crowing of the cock, the Delegated Officer shall be reverently waiting at the outside of the Chau Hâng gate. An officer of the Sacrificial Court shall then dispatch the proper person to reverently invite the Imperial Heaven, Ruler Above's divine tablet forth, and place it within the tent, and also arrange before it, one sacrificial bundle of silk, one wine vessel, three cyathi, one furnace, two candlesticks, the hams of a deer, some minced venison, some minced rabbit, and five kinds of fruit. Trays of roasted animals shall not be needed, neither shall there be any music. Two ushers of the Sacrificial Court shall lead the Delegated Officer within the right door of the Chau Hâng gate, and through the right south gate of the outer enclosure, and there through the right south gate of the inner enclosure, bring him to the Round Hillock, which he shall ascend by the west steps unto the third terrace, and from there by the main steps go up to the front of the worshipping place, where he shall stand facing north. The ceremonial officer shall then cry. "All ye attendant officers see that ye, each of you, do your respective duties." (Hereafter from the receiving of the god until the watching of the burning, it pertains to the duty of the ceremonial officer to issue the necessary calls). The ushers shall then lead the Delegated Officer to his worshipping place, where he shall stand and there receive the god. The incense mandarin shall now take his censer and enter. The master of ceremonies having issued the call to ascend the altar, shall lead the Delegated Officer by the west steps up to the first terrace unto the incense table. The incense mandarin shall kneel and offer the incense. The master of ceremonies shall cry "kneel" the Delegated Officer shall kneel, cry, "offer incense," the Delegated Officer shall offer a stick of incense, then on the second time, and on the third sliced sandlewood and then arise. Then it shall be cried "return to your place," whereupon the Delegated Officer shall be led down the west steps to his original place. Then it shall be cried, "kneel," "kow-tow," "arise." (Hereafter all formalities connected with ascending the altar, returning to ones place and other ceremonies, shall be announced by a crier) whereupon the Delegated Officer shall kneel three times, and kow-tow nine times. Then should come the ceremonies of presenting the sacrificial bundle of silk, and the first (drink) offering. The officer in charge of the sacrificial bundle of silk, bearing his basket, and the officer in charge of the cyathus carrying the cyathus shall now successively enter. The Delegated Officer shall now mount the altar, and approach before the shrine of the Ruler Above. The officer in charge of the sacrificial bundle of silk, shall kneel and offer the basket, the Delegated Officer shall likewise kneel, receive the basket, and place it upon the table. Then the cyathus bearer shall kneel, and offer the cyathus. The Delegated Officer shall kneel receive the cyathus, reverently offer it, pour a libation in the middle, and then arise. The officer in charge of the ritual shall then approach before the ritual table, kneel, kow-tow three times, respectfully receive the ritual tablet and then kneel to the left of the table. The ushers shall then lead the Delegated Officer from the first terrace down the right side of the middle steps, to the second terrace, to his place for listening to the reading of the ritual, where he shall kneel facing North. The ritual officer having finished the reading of the ritual, shall approach before the shrine of the god, kneel, place it back in the table, kow-tow as before, and then retire. The Delegated Officer shall kow-tow three times, and descend by the west steps to his place. Then shall come the second (drink) offering, in which the libation is poured to the left. This is to be followed by the last (drink) offering, in which the libation is to be poured in the right, with exactly the same rites in each case. Then the god is to be dismissed, while the Delegated Officer shall kneel three times and kow-tow nine times. The proper officers shall then receive successively the ritual, the sacrificial bundle of silk, and the incense, and reverently take them to the burning place. The Delegated Officer shall turn and stand on the west side of his worshipping place facing East, to watch them pass. Having resumed his proper position, he shall be led without the right south gate of the inner enclosure, to the place for watching the burning, where he shall stand to witness the burning. The accomplishment of all the rites having been announced, he shall be led out by the right south gate of the outer enclosure. An officer of the Sacrificial Court shall then direct the proper officer to reverently invite the tablet of the god back to its Imperial place, after which all shall retire."

TRANSLATION OF THE CHINESE RITUAL ON THE PRAYER FOR GRAIN.

"All ceremonies connected with prayer on behalf of grain, must take place on the South Common, North of the Round Hillock, on an altar constructed with three terraces, on the top one of which shall be raised a temple to be called "Prayer for the Year." Yearly, on the first lin of the first month, sacrifice shall be offered to the Ruler Above, on behalf of the common people to beseech for a good harvest. The shrine of Imperial Heaven, Ruler Above, shall be in the first (topmost) terrace, within the temple, facing South. The (deceased) Emperors T'ai Tsu Kao (T'ien Ming, 1616), Tai Tsung Wên (T'ien Tsung, 1627), Shih Tsu Chang (Shun Chih, 1644), Shing Tsu Jên (Kang Hi, 1662), and Shih Tsung Hien (Yung Chêng, 1723), shall be associated with him, having their places facing East and West. The day previous to the sacrifice, the Emperor shall go to the South Common to fast and sleep. When he shall have arrived at the right side of the south gate of the outer enclosure of the Prayer-on-behalf-of-grain-altar, he shall dismount from his chariot. Two ushers of the Sacrificial Court shall then lead the Emperor within the left door of the Prayer-for-the-Year gate, unto the Imperial Heaven temple, when he shall offer incense and worship. He shall then go to the Prayer-for-the-Year temple, to reverently inspect the shrines of the altar. When that is done, he shall pass through the east gate unto the Treasury of the gods, to inspect the baskets and trenchers, and also the stalls of the sacrificial animals. When done, he shall go to the Hall of fasting. On the day of the sacrifice, the Emperor's worshipping place shall be set up in the first (topmost) terrace within the temple door. The position for hearing the ritual and receiving the happiness (wine) and roast meats, shall be in front of the worshipping place. The Emperor shall enter the left door of the Prayer-for-the-Year gate, ascend by the left steps, and enter the left door of the temple unto his worshipping place, where he shall worship. The position of the royal relations assisting on the sacrifice shall be in the first terrace without the temple, at the head of the steps. The position of the numerous civil and military officers shall be in the third terrace, at the foot of the steps. The head of the Board of Rites shall now dispatch an officer of the Sacrificial Court, to go to the Imperial Heaven temple to reverently write the tablets, of the gods out and place them within the temple of Prayer-for-the Year. Before the Ruler Above shall be used one sacrificial bundle of silk, music and whole burnt offerings shall be employed to receive the Ruler god, the band to play the Praying for Peace air. At the presenting of the Imperial sacrificial bundle of silk, the Steady Peace air shall be played. When the sacrificial bowl is carried in, the Ten Thousand Peace air shall be played. At the first (drink) offering, the Precious Peace air. The second (drink) offering, the Luxuriant Peace air. The final (drink) offering, the Felicitous Peace air. At the removing of the dishes the Enriched Peace air. At the dismissal of the Ruler god, the Fruitful Peace air. At the watching of the burning, the Grain Peace air. When the Rites shall have been accomplished, the head of the Board of Rites shall dispatch an officer of the Sacrificial Court, to reverently invite the tablets of the gods to return unto the royal Imperial Heaven temple. All the rest of the ceremonies shall be just like those of the Round Hillock."

TRANSLATION OF THE RITUAL AT THE SACRIFICE IN PRAYER FOR RAIN.

"All ceremonies connected with the usual Prayer for rain. A sacrifice to Imperial Heaven, Ruler Above, at the Round Hillock, to pray for a fruitful rain in behalf of the one hundred kinds of grain, shall take place yearly, in the fourth month, when the dragon star has appeared, on a day selected by divination. On the day previous to the sacrifice, the Emperor shall fast and sleep at the South Common. He shall also enter the Circular Hall of the Imperial Expanse to offer incense, go to the Round Hillock to inspect the shrines of the altar, enter the treasury of the gods to look after the baskets and trenchers, and inspect the stalls of the sacrificial animals. On the day of the sacrifice the shrines of Imperial Heaven, Ruler Above, of the Associated Ones, of the Secondary Participators, shall be set up exactly as at the Great Sacrifice on the Winter solstice. Before the Ruler Above, shall be used only one sacrificial bundle of silk, as in the case of prayer on behalf of grain. Music and whole burnt offerings shall be employed to receive the ruler god, the band to play the Cloudy Peace air. At the presenting of the Imperial sacrificial bundle of silk, the Cloud Peace air shall be played, when the sacrificial bowl is carried in, the Necessary Peace air. At the first (drink) offering the Soaking Peace air shall be prayed. At the second (drink) offering, the Dew Peace air. At the final (drink) offering, the Drizzling Peace air. When removing the dishes, the Spirit Peace air. At the dismissal of the Ruler god the Steeped Peace air. When watching the burning the Drenching Peace air. The rest of the rites are exactly like those of the Great sacrifice on the Winter solstice."

TRANSLATION OF THE RITUAL AT THE SACRIFICE, WITH THE EXTRAORDINARY PRAYER FOR RAIN.

"All ceremonies connected with the Extraordinary Prayer for rain. If it should not rain after the ordinary yearly prayer for rain in the fourth month, a Delegated Officer should be sent to reverently inform the Celestial gods, the terrestrial gods, and the Great Year (god). Should it not rain then after seven days, the gods of the land and grain should be informed. If it still does not rain the celestial and terrestrial gods and the Great Year (god) should be informed again. If after this third time it should not rain, then the Extraordinary Prayer for rain shall take place. The day previous to offering the Extraordinary Prayer for rain, an officer shall be delegated to reverently inform the Imperial Ancestors. On this same day also at 9 o'clock A.M., the Emperor dressed in his ordinary clothes, shall go to the Hall of Fasting. There shall be no music, no cleaning of the streets, and no cries to clear the way. On the day of the sacrifice wearing a rain hat and plain clothes, he shall personally make known his request at the Round Hillock where he shall have set up the shrine of Imperial Heaven, Ruler Above, and those of the four Secondary Participators. All the royal relatives and those beneath them in rank assisting in the sacrifice shall likewise be dressed in rain hats and plain clothing. When the three (drink) offerings shall have been offered, and the music stopped, the respective sixteen dancing youths dressed in dark green clothes, shall perform the royal exercise with feathers and fans and sing the eight milky-way hymns composed personally by the Emperor to pray for a good heavy rain. The rest of the rites, together with the musical airs, shall be exactly like those of the Ordinary Prayer for rain. Should it rain then let another sacrifice be offered under the care of a Delegated Officer dressed in official robes who shall perform all the rites as in ordinary occasions. If it should rain after the fast, but before the sacrifice, another sacrifice shall take place as in the former case."

TRANSLATION OF THE CHINESE RITUAL FOR THE SACRIFICE TO EARTH. THE IMPERIALLY AUTHORIZED EDITION OF THE COLLECTED STATUTES OF THE GREAT PURE DYNASTY. SECTION 38TH.

Board of Rites. Bureau of Sacrifices. Great Sacrifice, No. 2. All sacrificial rites to Earth must take place on the North Common, where, because it is the place of the female principle, (Yin) an altar shall be erected to be called the Square Pool. It shall consist of two terraces, and at the four extremes of it, there shall be square pits to collect water. Here on the day of the summer solstice, is to be offered a sacrifice to Imperial Earth, the Producer. To this sacrifice, as equal sharers, are to be invited Emperor T'ai Tsu Kao, (T'ien Ming, 1616), Emperor T'ai Tsung Wên (T'ien Tsung, 1627), Emperor Shih Tsu Chang (Shun Chih, 1644), Emperor Sheng Tsu Jên (Kang Hi, 1662) and Emperor Shih Tsung Hien (Yung Ching, 1723); and as secondary participators, the five high mountains, the five marts, the four oceans, the four rivers, and the five hills Ch'i Yun, T'ien Chu, Lung Yeh, Chăng Zhui and Yung Ning. The place of Imperial Earth, the Producer, shall be on the first (topmost) terrace, facing North; that of the respective Holy Ones facing East and West. The positions of the four classes of Secondary Participators, shall be on the second terrace; the five High mountains and three hills, Ch'i

Yun, T'ien Chu and Yung Ning facing West, with the four Oceans next to them; the five Marts and the two hills, Lung Yeh and Ch'ang Zhui facing East, with the four Rivers next to them. All these shall be covered with yellow tents. Before Imperial Earth, the Producer, shall belong a yellow jade badge (much used during the Chen dynasty to denote princely rank, it has eight corners with a round hole in the center, and its shape was thought to resemble the earth) one sacrificial bundle of silk, 1 calf, 1 platter, 2 hampers (square outside and round within), 2 hampers (round outside and square within), flat baskets and trenchers 12 of each, 1 wine vessel, 3 cyathi, 1 furnace, and 4 candlesticks. Before the respective Holy Ones shall belong, equally, 1 sacrificial bundle of silk, 1 calf, 1 platter, the two kinds of hampers 2 of each, flat baskets and trenchers 12 of each, 1 wine vessel, 3 cyathi, 1 furnace, and four candlesticks. Before each of the Secondary Participators shall belong 1 sacrificial bundle of silk, while before each tent shall belong, equally, 1 cow, 1 sheep, 1 pig, 1 platter, 2 sacrificial broth jars, the two kinds of hampers two of each, flat baskets and trenchers ten of each, 1 wine vessel, 3 cyathi, 30 wine cups, 1 furnace and two candlesticks. The Imperial sacrificial bundle of silk, shall be placed in the baskets, the sacrificial animals in the trays, the wine vessels shall be full of wine, and coarse cloths shall cover the spoons. The day previous to the sacrifice, the Board of Music shall place in readiness the musical instruments for playing the harmonious airs of Shun under the altar, hanging them in the right and left. The Imperial Guard shall arrange the state traveling equipage outside of the Palace, and place the Golden chariot at the foot of the steps of the Great Peace gate. A 9 o'clock A.M., an officer of the Sacrificial Court shall go to the Kien T'sing (Heavenly Pure) gate, and memorialize the Emperor to go to the Hall of Fasting. The Emperor shall then put on his Imperial dragon embroidered robes, ascend the ceremonial chair, and depart from the Palace. There shall be the retinue of household Lords and Imperial Guards to proceed and follow him as is customary. When the bottom of the steps of the Great Peace gate is reached, the Emperor shall leave the chair and mount the Imperial chariot. When the procession starts, all persons are to be warned off the road. The bell of the Palace shall then be rung, and while the Imperial equipage is moving off, those members of the Imperial family and all those civil and military officials, who are not going to assist in the sacrifice, being dressed in official robes shall all kneel to see it depart. The musicians of the procession shall be there, but shall not play, an orderly of the Imperial Guard, however, shall ring the bell of the Hall of Fasting. When the Emperor has entered the West gate of the Altar, and arrived at the outside of the North gate of the Square Pool, he shall descend from his chariot, whence two ushers of the Sacrificial Court shall reverently lead the Emperor through the right hand door within unto the Imperial Producer House, when before Imperial Earth, the Producer, and before the respective Holy Ones, he shall offer incense, and thereafter kneel three times and worship (kow-tow) nine times.

Before the positions of the Secondary Participators, a delegated sacrificial officer shall be sent to offer incense and perform the rites. Then the Emperor shall go to the Square Pool, and look at the tablet places of the altar; then go to the treasury of the god, and look at the baskets and trenchers, and the stables of the sacrificial animals, when done, he shall leave by the right North gate of the inner enclosure, and through the right North gate of the outer enclosure go out to the left side of the road of the gods, when he shall ascend the Imperial chariot and proceed to the Hall of Fasting. Those members of the Imperial family and those numerous officers, who are to assist in the sacrifice, dressed in their official robes, shall all assemble outside of the Hall of Fasting, and then divided into companies, reverently watch the Emperor enter and then retire. On the day of the sacrifice when it is one hour and three quarter before sunrise, an officer of the Sacrificial Court shall enter the Hall of Fasting, to tell the time. The Emperor shall then put on his Imperial sacrificial robes, and having entered his ceremonial chair go out, then leaving his chair he shall mount his chariot, while an orderly of the Imperial Guards rings the bell of the Hall of Fasting. When the Emperor has arrived at the outside of the North gate of the outer enclosure, at the left side of the road of the gods, he shall dismount from his chariot, whence two ushers of the Sacrificial Court shall reverently lead him within the great waiting place, to wait while the head of the Board of Rites shall dispatch some officer of the Sacrificial Court to enter the Imperial Producer's House, and reverently invite the tablet of the god out; having placed it within the yellow tent, the officer of the Sacrificial Court shall then memorialize the Emperor to perform the rites. The Emperor shall then leave the great waiting place and wash, after which the ushers of the Sacrificial Court shall reverently lead the Emperor through the right North gate of the outer enclosure, in through the right North gate of the inner enclosure, up the main steps to the second terrace yellow tent waiting place, where he shall stand before the worshipping place there. A master of ceremonies of the Sacrificial Court, shall then lead the four delegated sacrificial officers, entering by the left North gate, to the raised middle walk at the front of the steps, where they shall stand. Officers of the Court of ceremonies shall then lead in the Imperial relations, who are to assist in the sacrifice, to their position at the foot of the steps, and the numerous mandarins to their position at the outside of the gate of the outer enclosure where they shall each take his place standing on the right and left and all facing the South. The ceremonial officer shall then call the musicians and mummers to sing a song, and the different attendants to attend to their respective duties. (Hereafter from the burying of the hair and blood until the removing of the dishes, it pertains to the duty of the ceremonial officer to issue the necessary calls). The eight bands of military performers shall enter, while the ushers shall memorialize the Emperor to take his position. The Emperor shall then take his worshipping place and stand, while the hair and blood is buried in the ground to receive the gods. At the same time the musical Director shall command the band to strike up the tune for receiving the god, viz., the air of Complete Peace. (All calls for music, from this time in, must be given through the musical director). Then the ushers shall cry "kneel," "worship," "arise," whereupon the Emperor shall kneel three times, and worship (kow-tow) nine times. The Imperial relatives and numerous officers shall all follow him in performing these rites. The incense bearers each carrying a censer, and the officers in charge of the Imperial sacrificial bundle of silk, each carrying a basket shall now enter, while the air of Wide Spread Peace is being played. Then the master of ceremonies shall cry "ascend the altar," whereupon, they shall reverently lead the Emperor to the first terrace before the shrine of Imperial Earth, the Producer. The incense bearers shall then kneel, and hold out the incense, the master of ceremonies shall then cry "kneel," the Emperor shall then kneel, cry, "offer incense," the Emperor shall then offer a stick of incense, "a second time" "a third time offering sliced sandlewood," "arise." The Emperor shall now approach before the table of the Imperial sacrificial bundle of silk, thereupon the officer in charge of the sacrificial bundle of silk, shall kneel and present the basket. The Emperor shall then kneel, receive the basket, place the Imperial sacrificial bundle of silk, and arise. After this he shall approach before the shrines of the respective Holy Associates, to offer incense and place the sacrificial bundles of silk, with the same rites. The master of ceremonies shall then cry "return to your place." (All the formalities of ascending the altar, returning to the original position, and the carrying out of the other ceremonies must be under the direction of a crier now and hereafter) the Emperor shall then return to his place. Then the bowls are to be brought in, thereupon the Emperor shall turn and stand at the side of his worshipping position, facing the West, while the proper officers shall pour the broth into jugs, and then reverently carry them from the bottom of the altar straight up the main steps to the shrine of Imperial Earth, the Producer, and to the shrines of the respective Holy Ones, where they shall kneel and hold them up, then arise and pour some of the broth into the bowls three times, after which they shall all retire, descending by the West steps. The Emperor then resumes his position. While the band plays the Full Peace air, the Emperor is to mount the altar and go before the shrine of Imperial Earth, the Producer, and before the shrines of the Associated Ones, where he shall kneel, offer the bowls, arise and then return to his place. The first of the (drink) offering ceremonies shall now take place. The Cyathi bearers, each carrying a cyathus shall now enter, the band to play the Great Peace air, and the martial performers to go through their exercise with shields and battle axes. The Emperor shall ascend the altar and go before the shrine of Imperial Earth, the Producer. The Cyathi bearers shall kneel and present their cyathi, the Emperor shall likewise kneel, offer the cyathi, pour libations in the middle, arise, go to the worshipping position which shall be his during the reading of the ritual, and stand there. The ritual officer shall then approach the ritual table, kneel, kow-tow three times, take up the ritual tablet, and kneel at the left of the table. The music shall now cease for a while. The Emperor shall then kneel, and likewise the whole company of mandarins. When the ritual officer has finished reading the ritual, he shall take the ritual tablet, approach before the shrine of Imperial Earth, the Producer, kneel, place it upon the table, kow-tow three times and retire, whereupon the music shall begin again. The Emperor shall now lead all his officers in worshipping (kow-towing) three times. When he has arisen, he shall go before the shrines of the Associated Ones and offer the cyathi successively with the same rites. The Master of Ceremonies shall then lead the delegated sacrificial officers to ascend the altar by the East and West steps, to the shrines of the Secondary Participators, to offer incense, to present sacrificial bundles of silk, and to successively offer the cyathi. When this is accomplished, they shall descend and retire to their original positions. The music shall again cease. The military performers shall now retire, while the eight bands of civil performers shall enter. The second of the (drink) offering ceremonies shall now take place, during the playing of the Tranquil Peace air, and the performance with feathers and fifes. The Emperor shall ascend the altar, offer successively the cyathi, pour libations to the left with the same rites as those of the first (drink) offering, and retire to his place. Then shall take place the ceremonies of the final (drink) offering during the playing of the Seasonable Peace air (the mummers' play to be the same as that of the second (drink) offering). The Emperor shall ascend the altar, offer successively the cyathi, pour libations to the right, with the same rites as those of the second (drink) offering, and then return to his place. The delegated sacrificial officers shall then offer the cyathi just as on the previous occasions. The music shall cease now, while the civil performers retire. An officer of the Sacrificial Court shall then cry "the bestowed happiness (wine) and roast meats." Two chief Butlers shall then approach the West table, take up the happiness (wine) and roast meats, enter before the shrine of Imperial Earth, the Producer, and hold them up. The Emperor shall then approach the drinking-their-happiness and getting-their-flesh worshipping place, and there stand. Two members of the Imperial Guard shall then enter and stand on the left. The officers in charge of the happiness (wine) and roast meats shall then descend and stand on the right. The Emperor is then to kneel, the right and left hand officers on duty shall each also kneel, whereupon the right hand officer shall present the happiness wine, the Emperor shall receive the cyathus, raise it up and pass it to the left hand officer. The roast meats shall be presented and received in the same manner. He then shall worship three times, arise, return to his place, and there lead all his officials in kneeling three times and worshipping (kow-towing) nine times. The dishes shall now be removed, while the band shall play the Pure Peace, air. An officer, whose duty it is, shall now approach before the shrine of Imperial Earth, the Producer, and take away the yellow jade badge and retire. The gods shall then be dismissed to the tune of Soothing Peace while the Emperor shall lead the whole band of his officers in kneeling three times, and worshipping (kow-towing) nine times. Officers, in charge, shall then remove successively the ritual, the sacrificial bundle of silk, the dishes, and the incense, and reverently take them to the burying pit, and also remove the sacrificial bundle of silk, dishes and incense belonging to the shrines of the Associated Ones, and reverently carry them to the burning place. The Emperor shall then change his position, standing at the side of his worshipping place facing West, to watch the ritual and sacrificial bundle of silk pass, after which he shall resume his old position. The incense and sacrificial bundle of silk belonging to the Secondary Participators shall likewise, by the east and west steps be carried to their respective burying places during the performance of music. When the sacrificial bundle of silk belonging to the Associated Ones are half burnt, the Emperor shall be memorialized to look at the burying, whereupon he shall be reverently led out through the right hand north gate of the inner enclosure to the place for watching the burying, there to witness the burying. The delegated sacrificial officials shall also respectively be led to the outside of the right and left hand gates, to witness the burying. It shall then be memorialized to the Emperor that the rites are over, whereupon, he shall be reverently led out through the right hand north gate of the outer enclosure into the great waiting place, where he shall change his clothes. Then the head of the Board of Rites shall dispatch an officer of the Sacrificial Court to reverently invite the tablet of the god to return to the royal Imperial Producer's House. When the Emperor has reached the outside of the north gate, he shall ascend the ceremonial chair. As the Imperial equipage proceeds, the musicians in the procession shall play the Protecting Peace air. When the Emperor returns home, he must be followed by his relatives, but the different mandarins may successively disperse. Those relatives and numerous officials, who did not assist at the sacrifice, shall be dressed in their official robes to kneel and receive the Emperor, outside of the Palace. While the Palace bell is ringing, the different relatives shall follow the Imperial chariot within unto the inner Gold Water bridge, where they shall reverently watch the Emperor enter the Palace, and then one and all disperse."

THE RITUAL FOR PRAYER TO EARTH ON ANY SPECIAL OCCASION.

"If for any reason a prayer to earth should be reverently offered, a delegated officer shall take charge of the service. The Sacrificial Court shall see that the yellow tents are put up in the Square Pool. An officer of the Sacrificial Court shall dispatch the proper officer to reverently invite the divine tablet of Imperial Earth the Producer, forth, and place it within the tent. The master of ceremonies of the Sacrificial Court shall lead the delegated officer in the left door of the north gate of the Square Pool, and through the left north gate of the outer enclosure enter the left north gate of the inner enclosure, unto the second terrace of the Square

Pool, to the worshipping place at the foot of the main steps, to carry out the rites. All ascending of the altar to offer incense, to present the sacrificial bundle of silk, and to pour out (drink) offerings, must be by the west steps. For the reading of the ritual, he must descend from first, terrace by the right hand side of the main steps to the reading-the-ritual-worshipping place, on the second terrace. All the goings-down to his regular position, shall, as usual, be by the west steps. All the remaining rites shall be just like those of Round Hillock, when prayer of like character is to be offered."

THE SACRIFICE TO EARTH.

Having thus presented a translation of the ritual for the sacrifice to Heaven and Earth, as the chief divinities of this worship, I come now to consider the text. In the "Collected Statutes" the sacrifice to Heaven is placed first in order; and that to Earth is second in order; but I will take up the explanation of the sacrifice to Earth first. This sacrifice is offered at the time of the summer solstice, on the altar to Earth, which is located on the north of the city, in a large open area, designated and preserved for this special purpose. This park is said to be only second to that in which the altar to Heaven is located. Connected with the altar to Earth there is a square pool, which is walled up with yellow bricks in reference to the color of the Earth. This pool is to be supplied with water at the time of offering the sacrifice. This sacrifice is offered to Deified Earth, or Earth considered as a god and the giver of great blessings. As in the case of idols, there is the external image which is the supposed representation of the spiritual Being connected with it, so in the worship of the objects of nature, there is a spiritual Being which is supposed to animate the visible object. The worshipper, in common language, is said, to worship *the visible object* whether it is an image or an object of nature. Earth as the object of worship is designated 地祇 Ti K'i. What the particular meaning of 祇 K'i in this connection is, has been with me, the subject of much inquiry. After much investigation I have come to the conclusion, that its meaning will be better expressed by the designation, The Producer than any other single term; but with the idea of nourishing also implied. Kang-hi in his Dictionary, copying from the Shwoh-wan defines Ti Ki as "the one who causes the myriad things to come forth."[1] This same definition is given in the Imperial Thesaurus. It is a common remark among the Chinese, that "Heaven is Father and Earth is Mother,"[2] which remark has reference to this early worship. The sentiment which assigns the functions of Mother to Earth favors the translation of Ki as the Producer. This definition of the deified earth by Kang-hi, shows that the very same idea was present in the nature worship in China as there was in Greece. Smith in his Classical Dictionary in the

---

[1] 地祇, 提出萬物者. (字典).　　[2] 天爲父, 地爲母. (諺語).

article Gaea or Earth, says, "Gaea belonged to the gods of the nether world. The surnames and epithets given to her, have more or less reference to her character as the all-producing and all-nourishing mother (mater omniparens et alma). At Rome, the earth was worshipped under the name of Tellus (which is only a variation of Terra)," page 271.

In the ritual, Earth has the same dignified adjective applied to it as is applied to Heaven. It is styled Imperial Earth. Dr. Legge has stated that this adjective was given to Heaven by Kea-tsing of the Ming Dynasty in the year 1535. I suppose that it was given to Earth with something of the same ceremonies as it was given to Heaven, at some time subsequent to that. But I have not been able to find out at what particular time. The sacrifice was formerly offered at an altar in the Park on the south of the city, which is still the altar to Heaven. But the grounds for the new park on the north of the city were prepared during this dynasty. Most probably at an early period in the reign of Kien-lung. He states in an imperial edict, referring to the park north of the city, in the 9th year of his reign, that the trees had not grown sufficiently to protect the retinue of officers and others, that accompanied the Emperor to the service, from the scorching sun. And again in an edict of the 11th year he says that the trees have grown so as to afford suitable protection from the heat. If any person can get a copy of a Book called "皇朝通典 Hwang Chiu T'ung tien," he would probably find when the adjective Imperial was given to Earth, and when the altar was removed to the north of the city. My efforts to get a copy of the work have been unsuccessful.

When the tablet with the title inscribed, Imperial Earth, the Producer, is brought out from the house where it is carefully kept during the intervening time, it is placed in a central position facing the North, in accordance with the doctrine of the Yin and the Yang. The tablets of the Imperial Ancestors of the reigning dynasty, are also brought forth from their sacred depository, and placed some facing the East, and some facing the West to the north of the tablet to the Earth, and on the same level with it, as the equal recipients of the sacrifice together with the Earth. That they are the equal and joint recipients of the sacrifice with the Earth, appears evident from *three* things stated in the text. 1st, This is the correct rendering of the word 配 P'ei, which refers to their being present. 2nd, The text after giving in detail the offerings to be presented to Imperial Earth, then gives in like detail, the offerings which are to be presented to the Imperial Ancestors, and states that the Emperor, after he has gone through with the "three kneelings and nine prostrations" to Earth, gives the same worship to each one of the ancestral tablets. 3rd, As it is stated that the tablets of the gods of the five mountains, the five hills, the four seas and the four streams, which are parts of the Earth, are there as *secondary* participants in the sacrifice, it makes it all the *more clear* that the ancestors are there as co-principals, in receiving the sacrifice. The *secondary* recipients are said to be placed on a lower plane than the principals, as indicating this distinction. It is also further indicated by the fact that the worship is performed before them by some high official appointed for that purpose, and not by the Emperor himself.

In the official text of the sacrifice to Earth, the object worshipped is variously designated—sometimes it reads Imperial Earth, the Producer—sometimes Imperial Producer—sometimes the Square Pool and sometimes Shin 神 the god—is used—and all the terms which are applied to Earth and those which are applied to the Imperial Ancestors are placed on the same plane, to show the honor which is shown to them.

In the long lapse of the four thousand years during which we have the accounts of the worship of deified Earth, there have been various terms used to designate it. The constant and standard one is the sacrifice to Earth, the Producer—some of the other designations of Earth have been as follows:—神后 Shin hau, 后土 Heau t'ŏ, 社 Shie and 太社 T'a shie, and during the Han dynasty the imposing title 皇地后祇[1] was given to Earth. The altar for Earth has also had different designations, some of which are as follows; "square hillock," 方丘 that to Heaven being called the "round hillock;" "the great altar" 太折, but the present canonical designation is the square pool 方澤.

A close examination of the account of the sacrifices to Heaven and to Earth will show that one is the exact counterpart of the other. The worship in each service is rendered by the Emperor in person when possible. There is the same variety in the offerings which are presented. There are songs of praise sung at each service, and prayers are offered for blessings. I will now present some extracts from the Chinese Classics, from which will be seen, the light in which the Deified Earth has been regarded from the early times: and some extracts from the Imperial edicts and declarations of different Emperors showing their habitual recognition of the earth as a god. These authorities will fully explain why the sacrifice to Earth is in every thing the exact counterpart of that to Heaven.

In the Book of Rites, the following explanation is given of why the sacrifice to Earth is called 社 Shie. "This is by reason of the deification of the Earth. Earth contains all things, Heaven presents the appearances; supplies are obtained from Earth, rules are obtained from Heaven; hence we ought to honor Heaven and love Earth, and thereby teach the people to increase the thank-offering. The explanation says: 'We speak of recompensing the Shie's abundance, because *it* (the Earth) *has the same merit as Heaven.*' To increase the recompense is to make greater the thanks-giving ceremonies. The containing things—shows that the merit of Earth is the same as that of Heaven—therefore they appoint the Shie ceremony, and make it the same as the sacrifice to Heaven at the winter solstice—and truly give a worthy recompense to the [earth] god." The Tsieh-chi says. "If we obtain supplies, we have wherewith to nourish, nourishing is a mother's function; if we obtain rules, we have wherewith

---

[1] 今宜地祇稱皇地后祇,兆曰廣時.（杜佑通典）.

to teach, teaching is a father's function. That which heaven and earth manifest to men is excellent, therefore we ought to recompense them with that which is excellent."¹

In the Shoo King it is said "Heaven and Earth are the Father and Mother of all things." Dr. Legge in his note on this passage says, "by "all things" here we understand all things inanimate as well as animate." In one of the native commentaries, the following passages from the Yih King are quoted in explanation of this passage.. "How great is the originating virtue of Heaven, all things have their beginning from it;" "How great is the originating virtue of earth, all things were produced by it; it is the complaisant help mate of Heaven."² The Yih King also says. "K'ien is Heaven, therefore we style it father, K'wan is earth, therefore we style it mother."³ "First there are Heaven and Earth, and then all things are produced."⁴ "Heaven and Earth exert their influences and all things are produced."⁵ "The great virtue of Heaven and Earth is to produce."⁶ "Heaven and Earth nourish all things."⁷ T'so chuen says "Imperial Heaven and Sovereign Earth truly hear what the King says."⁸ Chau-tsz says, "When Heaven and Earth are propitious, all things will be prosperous: therefore the Shěn and the Ki will be rendered gracious."⁹ This same idea is somewhat differently expressed in the Sze Ki. "When Heaven and Earth are happily harmonious, and the Yin and the Yang are mutually efficacious, then the vivifying warmth and the substance, overshadow and nourish all things." On the explanation Chang Huen says: the vivifying warmth is called hü and the substance is called yü, and means, that Heaven and Earth by their fructifying effects overshadow and nourish all things."¹⁰ And again, "When Heaven and Earth are harmonious, the four seasons are,—seasonable."¹¹ In a commentary on the "Four Books" is the following ex-

1 郊特牲云，社所以神地之道也，地載萬物，天垂象，取財於地，取法於天，是以尊天而親地也，故教民美報焉，講解曰，言報社之隆，以其行同天之功也，美報者，善其報禮也，載物一段，見地之功同於天，故立社以禮之，使與郊天等，正以美報神之處也，又節旨曰，取財則有所發，發者母道也，取法則有所教，教者父道也，天地之所施於人者美矣，故不可不美其報. (見禮記備旨).

2 惟天地萬物父母，註，大哉乾元，萬物資始，至哉坤元，萬物資生，乃順承天，天地者，萬物之父母也. (書經監本註).

3 乾天也 故稱乎父，坤地也，故稱乎母. (易說卦).

4 有天地然後萬物生焉. (易經). 5 天地感而萬物化生. (易經).

6 天地之大德曰生. (易經). 7 天地養萬物. (易經).

8 皇天后土，實聞君之言. (左傳).

9 天地和則萬物順，故神祇格. (周子通書).

10 天地欣合，陰陽和得，煦嫗覆育萬物，註，鄭玄曰，氣曰煦，體曰嫗，言天地以氣體覆育萬物也. (史記樂書).

11 天地順而四時當. (史記).

planation of the Kiau and Shie worship or rites is given. "Kiau is the sacrifice to Heaven; Shie is the sacrifice to Earth." Chic Chung-tsze says: "The prayer in the spring for a good harvest, the great intercession for rain, in the summer, the thanks-giving in the fall, in the illustrious Hall, were all sacrifices to Heaven, but the sacrifice to Heaven at the winter solstice at the Round Hillock is the most important of all; so also the Li shie. The chau shie of the villages and the country's haw shie are all sacrifices to Earth, but the sacrifice to Earth at the summer solstice at the square pool is the most important of all."[1] The Book of Rites says: "Therefore the Emperor sacrifices to Heaven and Earth." The Commentary says: "The Heaven has the merit of overshadowing all things, the Earth has the merit of containing all things. The Emperor with heaven and earth is a trio, therefore the Emperor sacrifices to Heaven at the Round Hillock, and to Earth at the square pool."[2]

The ode says: "Heaven bestows, the Earth nourishes, hence the hundred grains grow abundantly."[3] The Book of Rites says: "According to Heaven, serve Heaven, according to Earth, serve Earth." The Commentary says: according to Heaven's elevation, and earth's depression, Heaven should be worshipped with flaming burnt offerings; and Earth should be worshipped by burying the animals on the ground, as at the summer and winter solsticial sacrifices."[4] The Chau Li says: "Use jade stone and make six vessels and offer to Heaven, Earth and the four quarters; the azure jade offer to Heaven, and the yellow to Earth." The explanation says: The pih should be in shape exactly *round* and *azure* to resemble Heaven. The tsung should be in shape eight cornered and yellow to resemble Earth."[5] "For I have heard that for the Emperor in person to sacrifice to Heaven and Earth is an ancient and present prevailing usage."[6] In the Li Tsi I it is said: "of things which Heaven has produced, and Earth nourished, there is nothing greater than man."[7]

And the Li Ki says: "The Emperor sacrifices to Heaven and Earth.

---

[1] 郊社之禮, 註, 郊祭天, 社祭地, 又儲中子曰, 春之祈穀, 夏之大雩, 秋之明堂, 均以祀天, 而惟冬至圜丘之典爲獨重, 遂之里社, 鄉之州社, 國之侯社, 均以祭地, 而惟夏至方澤之典爲特隆. (四書味根錄).

[2] 故天子祭天地, 解, 天有覆物之功, 地有載物之功, 天子與天地參, 故天子祭天於圜丘, 祭地於方澤. (禮記備旨).

[3] 天施地育分百穀蕃昌. (大淸圜丘樂章).

[4] 因天事天, 因地事地, 解, 因天地之尊卑, 而制燔柴祀天, 瘞牲事地之禮, 郊社是也. (禮記備旨).

[5] 以玉作六器以禮天地四方, 以蒼璧禮天, 以黃琮禮地, 註, 璧形正圓, 蒼象天也, 琮形八角, 黃象地也. (周禮春官.)

[6] 蓋聞天子親祀天地, 古今通禮也. (漢宣帝紀).

[7] 天之所生, 地之所養, 無人爲大. (禮記祭義).

The explanation reads: "Heaven and Earth are the greatest objects in the region; the Emperor is the most honorable in the kingdom, therefore he Sacrifices to Heaven and Earth."[1] Quotations of the same import as the above, might be multiplied indefinitely. But perhaps these are sufficient. I proceed to present some which represent the imperial acts and declarations of Emperors of successive dynasties.

The Emperor Tang, the first of the Shang dynasty, in his declaration says: "I therefore, a little child; charged with the decree of Heaven, and its bright terrors, did not dare to forgive. I used a dark colored animal and announced it to *Heaven above* and *to divine Earth*, and requested that they would consider Hea as a transgressor and punish him." Shoo King, p. 187. The Emperor Fah, the first of the Chaou dynasty says: "Hating the sins of Shang, I have announced to Imperial Heaven and Soverign Earth." Shoo King, p. 312. The first Emperor of the Sung dynasty Kien Teh in the first year of his reign sacrificed to *Heaven* and *Earth* at the Round Hillock."[2]

The first Emperor of Ta Tsing dynasty, Shun Chi, in the first year of his reign personally sacrificed to Heaven and Earth at the Southern suburbs. He says: "He ventures to announce to *Imperial Heaven* and *Soverign Earth*."[3] Hong Hi, the second Emperor of this dynasty, in an Imperial edict in the 36th year of his reign says: "I having determined that Kaldan should be punished, I sacrificed and announced to Heaven, Earth, and the ancestral temple and prayed that wherever my troops went Heaven above would protect and assist them."[4]

In December 1722, Kang Hi died after a reign of 61 years—on the next day after his death, the Peking Gazette published, as a most important document his lost testament. The Emperor, in this paper, after speaking of the length of his reign and his happiness, says he owes these things not to his own weak reason, "but to the invisible help of Heaven and of Earth, of my ancestors, and of the gods who preside over the Empire and over the land and the grain."[5] These words of Kang Hi are of special importance, as they, in a state paper, show what he regarded as the gods of his country.

The usual formula of announcement on all great matters of state; as a new Emperor ascending the throne, declaration of war, the death of an Empress, conferring a title on a deceased parent, or any additional title to a living mother is thus: "circumspectly sacrifice and announce to Heaven,

---

[1] 天子祭天地，解，天地，域之最大者，天子域中之至尊，故祭天地．(禮記備旨)．

[2] 宋太祖乾德元年，合祭天地於圜丘，將升壇，有司具黃褥爲道，上曰，朕潔誠事天，不必如此，命徹之．(宋史)．

[3] 大淸國皇帝臣御名，敢昭告於皇天后土．(順治元年郊天地祝文)．

[4] 朕以爲噶爾丹斷當急圖，遂祭告天地宗廟，我師所至，上天佑助．(康熙三十六年上諭)．

[5] 仰荷天地宗廟社稷默佑．(康熙上諭)．

to Earth, to the ancestral temple, to the gods of the land and of the grain."[1]

Quotations, showing the prominence which is given to the worship of Earth in the State Religion of China, might be greatly multiplied. But I close them here with a translation of an ode which is sung at the time of the summer solstice, when the service is concluded and the tablet of the god is about to return to the depository amidst the fragrance of the incense and the peals of the music. "The brilliant flags follow the cloudy way; the flying dragon mounts the high heaven; the virtues and actions of Earth are perfect; by thy care over all within the four seas there are no troubles; the Compeer of the imperial canopy, thou art one of the two great ones; thou dost keep in peace the people of the Earth below.[2] Thus it appears that the Heaven, the Earth, the Imperial ancestors and the gods of the land and the grain, (which gods are also the special protectors of each successive dynasty) are the objects to which the great sacrifices are respectively offered. It is also evident, from the language used in speaking of them, and from the worship and offerings given to them, that when the sun, moon and stars, the powers of nature, such as the winds, the clouds, the rain and the thunder; also when the mountains and the hills, the seas and the streams are sacrificed to, they are all considered as deified, and they are worshipped as gods.

THE SACRIFICE TO HEAVEN.

This sacrifice is offered to Heaven by the Emperor in person, after preparation by fasting, at the time of the winter solstice of each year, at the altar to Heaven in the Southern suburbs. The Emperor goes forth to attend to it in great state, attended by a large retinue of officials and guards and musicians. Nothing is absent from the ceremony which is adapted to make it imposing to the Chinese nation. The object to which the sacrifice is offered and the homage is given, is Heaven. The style of address which is now used, is Imperial Heaven. This honourable adjective was given—as Prof. Legge has stated, by Kiah Tsing, of the Ming dynasty, in the 17th year of his reign. This appellation had been used previously to that time, but had been in a great measure superseded by 昊天 Haou Tien. After what has been already written, I suppose very few will have any doubt but that the object then worshipped is the *visible Heavens* regarded as a *divinity*,—or *deified Heaven*. If any one does doubt it, then I submit this further proof. The word Heaven is used in designation of the object, in connection with the words earth, sun, moon, stars and the other objects of nature which are worshipped, without any indication that it is used in any other sense than they are, viz.: to indicate the object of nature usually so designated. Other words are also used to designate it which, if possible, indicate more distinctly the

---

[1] 謹祭告天地宗廟社稷. （道光登極詔又道光皇太后六旬萬壽詔又同治上兩宮皇太后尊號詔）.

[2] 靈旗兮雲路道，飛龍䡾兮高旻，陰儀粹兮德純，眷四海兮無塵，配皇穹兮兩大，綏下土兮蒸民. （大清祭地祇樂章）.

object which is intended. The object worshipped is often styled, "The canopied azure,"¹ thus indicating both its shape and its color. Sometimes it is styled "The high canopy,"² "The imperial canopy,"³ "The azure canopy,"⁴ "The azure heaven,"⁵ "The glorious azure,"⁶ "The heaven above, azure, azure,"⁷ "The azure above."⁸ The object which is worshipped is also represented by resemblances. The altar is made round designedly to represent the Heaven. There is near to the altar to Heaven, an imposing building of a dome shape and of a blue color which is called "The altar for prayer in behalf of grain," 祈穀壇 which prayer is offered to Heaven. The Building in shape and color resembles the blue vault of Heaven. The name of the southern chapel means, "The circular hall of the Imperial canopy." The jade stone gem, which is one of the things presented to Heaven at the time of offering the sacrifice, is required to be made "round and azure so as to resemble Heaven."⁹

The function of the object which is worshipped is also clearly expressed. "Heaven is said *to overshadow*, while earth *contains*."¹⁰ The one thus corresponds to the other. Heaven overshadows the things which the earth contains. Manifestly and beyond all contradiction *that which overshadows earth* is the visible Heavens. If these various words and resemblances and fuctions which are used to indicate the intended object of worship, do not render it evident beyond all doubt that the object sacrificed to is the *visible Heaven*, then it is impossible for human language to designate the visible Heaven. The worshipper of course regards this visible object *as a god*. And hence it is clear beyond all successful contradiction that deified Heaven and Earth are the two great objects of worship by the Emperor of China, in the state ceremonial.

These two great objects of worship are not only their chief gods, but they are the special protectors of the Empire and the Emperor. Hence it is said the Emperor regards Heaven as his Father, and Earth as his mother. And as the correlate of this, Heaven and Earth regard the Emperor as their son. The Emperor Kien Lung in his prayer for a plentiful year thus expresses himself. "The son of Heaven, &c., recognizes

---

1 雖有旅力, 以念穹蒼, 註, 穹蒼, 天也, 穹言其形, 蒼言其色. (詩經衍義).
2 傲高穹之大體以就乎陽. (鄭獬圜丘象天賦).
3 天所子兮眇躬, 予小子兮蒙降豐, 紛總總兮賴皇穹. (大清常雩樂章).
4 至治光華, 格於上下, 用能協應蒼穹, 嘉祥畢集. (乾隆十三年上諭).
5 蒼天蒼天, 視此驕人, 矜此勞人. (詩小雅巷伯之篇).
6 仰荷昊蒼眷佑, 壽越古稀. (乾隆祈穀上諭).
7 伍員仰天嘆曰, 我無瀝父, 無以至今日, 上天蒼蒼, 豈敢忘乎. (列國志).
8 仰荷上蒼眷佑, 中外蒙庥. (乾隆上諭).
9 以玉作六器以禮天地四方, 以蒼璧禮天, 註, 璧形正圓, 蒼象天也. (周禮春官).
10 故天子祭天地, 解, 天有覆物之功, 地有載物之功. (禮記備旨

Heaven as Father and Earth as mother; the reverently accepted duties, cannot be disregarded.¹" In the Han-yu it is said of the Tang Dynasty. "The Tang having received the command of Heaven to be Heaven's son [*i.e.* Emperor], all the kingdoms of the four regions were submissive and obedient to the dynasty.² "In the Hwang-chiu, one of the odes expresses the feelings of the Emperor thus, "He whom Heaven recognizes as son, is my unworthy self. I, a mere child, with reverential awe, invoke you to send a bountiful year, for all creatures rely on the Imperial canopy.³" In the Tung Tien, it is said, that the kings recognize Heaven as Father, and Earth as mother.⁴

At the sacrifice to Heaven, the Imperial ancestors are the participants with Heaven in receiving the sacrifice. The tablet to Heaven face the South and the tablets to the ancestors are arranged some facing to the East and some toward the West according to their respective rank. When it is considered that the Emperor is the Son of Heaven and Earth, it is not so strange that the deified Imperial earthly ancestors are thus brought forth to be the participators with Heaven and Earth at the sacrifice offered to each respectively. The sun, moon and stars, together with the gods of the winds and the clouds, the rain and the thunder are the secondary participators in the sacrifice. The services, in the offerings, the worship, the prayers, and the hymns of praise, are in all respects the counterpart to those which occur in the sacrifice to Earth,

To us who have been taught from our childhood to regard the true God, Jehovah, as a *Spiritual* Being possessing all divine attributes and all power in Heaven and Earth, it appears very strange that the human mind can be so darkened as to ascribe the attributes and works of Jehovah to any other Being, whether that Being may be a so-called immortal god, or a deified object of nature. But the whole history of idolatrys and the observation of those who live among a heathen people, show that the heathen recognize a *personality* and *intelligence*, and the *exercise of power*, as belonging to every object, whatever it may be, that they deify. Many of the heathen pray to the so-called Goddess of Mercy, with the same sincerity and belief in her power to grant mercy, as the Christian prays to the true and only Saviour. The various nations of antiquity trusted in, and acknowledged their respective chief god to be their special protector, as earnestly as did the Israelites trust in and acknowledge Jehovah to be their God. So the Chinese people in all ages have ascribed, personality, intelligence and power to deified Heaven and Earth. They have received it as a truth, that Heaven had the absolute and entire control of every thing relating to the government of China; the

---

1 天子父天母地, 祗承之義, 不可稍弛. (乾隆祈穀上諭).
2 唐受天命為天子, 凡四方萬國, 咸臣順於朝. (韓愈送殷員外文).
3 天所子兮眇躬, 予小子兮凜降堙, 紛總總兮頼皇穹. (大清常雩樂章).
4 王者父天母地.(通典).

right of appointing the rulers of the country, of displacing those who had disregarded the command of Heaven, and oppressed the people—the granting of fruitful seasons and the products of the Earth—the infliction of national calamities in punishment of national sins, &c., &c. While the government has suffered the idolatries of Taouism and Buddhism to spread among the people, and while some of the Emperors of different dynasties have given special encouragement to one or other of these false religions, as they are styled by the Confucianists, yet during this long period of four thousand years, the government has retained, in wonderful uniformity, the services of the state religion free from any change or corruption. It is therein a striking commentary on the words of Jeremiah to the Jews when he asks: "Hath a nation changed their gods which are yet no gods." Jer. 2: 11, and again "For all people will walk every one in the name of his God." Mic. 4: 5. The Chinese books are abundant in passages setting forth the power and rule of Heaven and his beneficence to the Chinese people. I will present only a few out of the many that are at hand. In the Shoo King at page 153 of Dr. Legge's translation, one of the Emperor's of the Hea Dynasty going to war against a rebellious vassal says: "On this account Heaven is about to destroy him (the vassal) and bring to an end the favor it has shown to him; and I am reverentially executing the punishment appointed by Heaven." Chung hwui of the Shang Dynasty announces thus: "Heaven gives birth to the people with such desires, that without a Ruler, they must fall in to all disorders; and Heaven again gives birth to the man of intelligence whose business it is to regulate them. * * Heaven gifted our king with valor and wisdom to continue the old ways of Yaou. You are now only following the standard course, honoring and obeying the appointment of Heaven. The king of Hea was an offender, falsely pretending to the sanction of supreme Heaven." Shoo, pp. 178-9. In the Shoo King, the Emperor Yaou said to Shun when he wanted him to occupy the throne with him, "The *determinate appointment* of Heaven (to be Emperor) rests upon your person; you must eventually ascend the throne of the great sovereigns: p. 61. "The way of Heaven is to bless the good and to punish the bad. It sent down calamities on the house of Hea to make manifest its crimes." Therefore I (the little child, charged with the decree of Heaven did not dare to forgive the criminal. I used a dark colored animal, and making a clear announcement to Heaven above and sovereign Earth, requested them to deal with Hea as a criminal." pp. 186-7. "The King on succeeding to the throne, did not follow the advice of Ahang. E Yin then made the following writing. "The former king kept his eye continually upon the bright requirements of Heaven, and served the spirits (gods) of Heaven and Earth, of the land and the grain, and of the ancestral temple. Heaven took notice of his virtue, and caused his great appointment to light upon him." p. 199. "Great Heaven has graciously favored the house of Shang, and granted to you, O young King, at last to become virtuous." p. 206. E Yin said: "Oh it is difficult to rely on Heaven: its appointments are not constant. If the sovereign virtue is constant, he will preserve his throne. The King of Hea could not maintain the virtue of his ancestors unchanged, but contemned the spirits [gods] and oppressed the people. Great Heaven no longer extended its protection to him. * * * Then were E Yin and T'ang possessed of virtue and able to satisfy the mind of Heaven. He received the bright favor of Heaven, and became the Master of the nine provinces: * * * it was not that Heaven had any partiality for Shang; Heaven simply gave its favor to pure virtue." p. 214-16. "It is Heaven which is all-intelligent and observant. Let the sage King take it as his pattern; then his ministers will reverently accord with him:" p. 255. O King, you are bringing on the end yourself, on this account Heaven has cast us off.* * * Our people now all wish the dynasty to perish saying, "Why does not Heaven send down its indignation? Why does not some one with its great decree make his appearance. What has the present King to do with us. The King said Oh! is not my life secured by the decree of Heaven? Tsoo E, returned and said, Ah! Your crimes which are many are set above: and can you speak of your fate as if give it in charge to Heaven?" pp. 271-2. An emperor of the Chow Dynasty which succeeded the Shang, says: "The iniquity of Shang is full, Heaven gives command to destroy it. If I did not comply with Heaven, my iniquity would be as great.* * I have received charge from my deceased Father Wān: I have offered special sacrifice to Shangti; I have performed the das services to great Earth; and I lead the multitude of you to execute the punishment appointed by Heaven. Heaven compassionates the people. What the people desire, Heaven will be found to give effect to." pp. 287-8. "Heaven loves the people, and the sovereign should reverence Heaven. Keih, the sovereign, could not follow the example of Heaven.* * * Heaven favored and charged T'ang, the successful, to make an end of the decree of Heaven.* * * It would seem that Heaven is going by means of me, to rule the people. My dreams coincide with my divinations; the auspicious omen is double." pp. 290-1. "Heaven sees as my people see, Heaven hears as my people hear." p. 292. "He neglects the sacrifice to Heaven and Earth. He has discontinued the offerings in the ancestral temple." p. 295. "Do ye support with untiring zeal me, the one man, reverently to execute the punishment appointed by Heaven." p. 296. "On the day ting-we, he sacrificed in the ancestral temple of Chow. * * * Three days after he presented a burnt offering to Heaven and worshipped toward the mountains and the rivers, solemnly announcing the successful completion of the war." p. 300. "Detesting the crimes of Shang, I announced to great Heaven and sovereign Earth, to the famous hill and the great hill by which I passed.* * * Reverently obeying the determinate counsel of Heaven, I pursue my punitive work to the end, to give tranquility to its men and women, "p. 314. "In the autumn, when the grain was abundant and ripe, but before it was reaped, Heaven sent a great storm of thunder and lightning, along with wind, by which the grain was all beaten down and great trees torn up. * * Now Heaven has displayed its terrors to display the virtue of the Duke of Chow. The King then went out to the borders, when Heaven sent down rain: and by virtue of a contrary wind the grain all rose up," pp. 359-60. "Great Heaven having given the Middle Kingdom with its people and territories to the former kings, do you, our present sovereign, employ your virtue, effecting a gentle harmony among the deluded people, leading and urging them on; so also will you please the former kings who received the appointment from Heaven," p. 418. Such passages might be quoted to any extent out of the Shoo-king. But perhaps this is sufficient. Those who are interested in pursuing the subject will consult it for themselves—as this Book is in the hands of most Chinese scholars, I do not copy out the Chinese text, of the above quoted passages. This same style of speaking in regard to the change of dynasties, and the setting up of the Rulers in this Empire, continues to the present time. "The first Emperor of this dynasty made the announcement to Heaven and Earth,"[1] ascribed the obtaining of the kingdom to Heaven. Kang Hi, when he obtained the victory over the Kaldan, on the 36th year of his reign, ordered a thanksgiving to Heaven. He also ascribes the prosperity of his reign "to the invisible help of Heaven, Earth, his ancestors and the gods of the land and the grain."[2]

Each one of the successive Emperors, when he ascends the throne, "announces the important event to Heaven, Earth, the Imperial ancestors and to the gods of the land and of grain."[3] Very many more passages with such statements as these from the classics, and other standard works and from the Collected Statutes of this present dynasty, are in my possession. But the passages already quoted are more than sufficient to satisfy every candid mind that the great gods of the Chinese Government are Deified Heaven and Earth, and that the Imperial ancestors and the Shie Tsik, the gods of the land and the grain, are associated with them as objects of Imperial worship and service, in the state religion of the empire.

I come to the translation of 皇天上帝 which I regard as the most important phrase in the whole ritual. I have translated it "Imperial Heaven, *The Ruler* above." I have translated it thus as expressing the obvious sense of the phrase, as required by the grammatical construction; and as supported by the highest authorities, both Chinese and Foreign. This is to me the *obvious* meaning of the sentence. For we have seen above that the *object* sacrificed to is the visible Heaven *regarded as a god.* We have also seen that to deified Heaven all power and rule are ascribed. These ideas are expressed in the translation "Imperial Heaven, the Ruler above." This translation is also in accordance with plain *grammatical construction*, as the first noun refers to the object sacrificed to, *the positive*

---
[1] 大淸國皇帝臣(御名)敢昭告於皇天后土 (順治元年郊天地祝文)
[2] 仰荷天地宗廟社稷默佑, (康熙上諭).
[3] 謹祭告天地宗廟社稷, 見道光登極詔.

object *Heaven,* and the second noun, Ruler, is in opposition with the first, as expressing the great function of Heaven "*the Ruler above.*"

In reference to deified Earth, we saw that as "the mother of all things" it is very properly designated "The Producer." Deified Heaven is designated "the Father of all things." By the common consent of mankind of all ages, the function of ruling and governing the family pertains to the Father. So likewise, the Chinese people having designated Heaven "the Father of all things," have ascribed to it the function of ruling and governing all things; and as expressive of this function thus ascribed to Heaven, it is designated "The Ruler above." The Chinese writers all concur in this explanation.

The Chinese authorities thus define and explain the words Shangti. Kang Hi explains Shangti "as being the same as Heaven." The Book of History has the same statement. "Shangti is Heaven.¹" In the Fung-Shen Book it is said that, "Shangti is another name for Heaven.²" In the explanation of a passage in the Shoo where Heaven and Shangti are used interchangeably, we have an explanation why they are so used.—The passage of the Shoo reads: "When T'ang the successful, had received the favoring decree, he had with him E Yin whose virtue was able to affect great Heaven. T'ao Mow had E Chin and Chin Hoo, whose virtue was able to affect Shangti." p. 478. The explanation reads. "When we speak in reference to its *overshadiug all things* we call it *Heaven;* when we speak in reference to its *ruling and governing*, we call it *Ti*, (or Ruler.) In the Books whether it is *styled Heaven or Ruler*, the one or the other is used according *to what is referred to,* and these designations are *alike honorable.*"³ The passage in the Shoo, page 179, which also has Heaven and Ruler used interchangeably reads thus; "The King of Heaven was an offender, falsely pretending to the sanction of Heaven above to spread abroad his commands among the people. On this account Ti [the Ruler] viewed him with disapprobation." The commentary in explanation of Heaven and Ruler, says: "On account of *its form and substance* it is called Heaven, and on account of *its ruling* and *governing* it is called Ruler.⁴" I may remark that *every where* in the classics, and the commentaries on them, "Ruler above," and "Ruler" are used interchangeable. In the ode Ching yneh of the Shi King, there occurs the expression. "There is the great Ruler above." The explanation reads; "'hwang' means great—Shangti is the Heaven-god. Ching Tsze says, in reference *to its form and substance,* we call it Heaven; *in reference to its*

1 上帝, 天也, 字典又史記正義.
2 上帝者, 天之別名也, 封禪書宗祀文王於明堂以配上帝句註.
3 時則有若伊尹, 格於皇天, 時則有若伊陟臣扈, 格於上帝, 註, 自其徧覆言之謂之天, 自其主宰言之謂之帝, 書或偁天, 或稱帝, 各隨所指, 非有軒輊也, 書經監本註.
4 夏王有罪, 矯誣上天, 以布命於下, 帝用不臧, 註, 矯與矯制之矯同, 誣, 罔也, 天以形體言, 帝以主宰言. （書經監本註）

ruling and *governing we call it Ruler.*"¹ In the Li Ki......it reads: "The Emperor (*i.e.* The son of Heaven) is about to go forth and sacrifice to the Ruler above." The Chih chi explains "to offer sacrifice to Shangti, is to sacrifice to Heaven."² In the *Shu King* we find the following passage "The people suffering from cruel oppression and murderous slaughter plead their innocence on high, and asked the Ruler above to look down on the people, but they have no acceptable virtue." The explanation reads: "cruel oppression on the part of the sovereign, leads to numerous executions among the people: whereupon the people plead their innocence before Heaven; Heavens looks down upon the people of Min, but they have no acceptable virtue."³ In the Shoo, at p. 286, we have this remarkable passage—"Heaven, to protect the people below, made for them rulers and made for them instructors, that they might be aiding to the Ruler above and secure the tranquility of the four quarters of the Empire." The commentary reads: "It says that Heaven out of regard to the people below, established rulers to govern them, appointed instructors to teach them and the rulers and the instructors are able to help the Ruler above."⁴

These passages, it appears to me, express the meaning as clear as human language can express the ideas of a people, that in regard to deified Heaven, when the *object* thus worshipped is referred to, it is called Heaven, and that when *its function* as the Ruler and Governor of all things is referred to, then it is designated "*The Ruler above.*" From this it follows, that Shangti is a designation applied to deified Heaven when it is referred to as the Ruler of all things. Heaven is the *positive existence* and the *divinity* which is worshipped, and Shangti, or Ruler above, is the designation applied to it as the Ruler of the Middle Kingdom, and governor and director of all its affairs. Hence come the various expressions as, the Son of Heaven 天子 to designate the Emperor. The Heaven conferred throne 天位, to designate the throne of China; The Heaven appointed punishments 天罰, to punishments which Heaven has decreed. The decrees of Heaven 天命, which are literally the decrees of deified Heaven. The Heaven appointed or established dynasty 天朝, meaning

有皇上帝. 註: 皇, 大也. 上帝, 天之神也. 程子曰, 以其形體謂之天, 以其主宰謂之帝. (詩經衍義)*

天子將出, 類乎上帝, 節言解, 類上帝, 祭天也. (禮記備旨)

³ 虐威庶戮, 方告無辜於上. 上帝監民, 罔有馨香德. 註, 虐政作威, 衆 庶敗戮者, 方各訴無罪於天, 天視苗民, 無有馨香德也. (書經監本註)

⁴ 天佑下民, 作之君, 作之師, 惟其克相上帝, 寵綏四方, 註, 言天眷佑 下民, 爲之君以長之, 爲之師以教之, 若師者, 惟其能助上帝, 以 愛安天下也. (書經監本註) 天之生成萬物, 而主宰之者謂之 帝. (康熙欽定易經註)

---

* Dr. Legge states that *this* explanation of the meaning of the designation of Heaven and Shangti as given by Ch'ing Tsze "*is accepted by Choo and all subsequent writers.*" See She King p. 316.

that each reigning dynasty has the throne by the appointment or Heaven. In all the classics, Shangti the Ruler above, and Ti, Rule, are used in common, the one for the other, and both are used interchangeable with Heaven. Dr. Legge, in his Prolegomena to the Shoo King says "We find The Ruler 帝 and the Supreme Ruler 上帝 constantly interchanged with Heaven," p. 193. Indeed the words Shangti, and its synonym Ti, have no other use, or application, in the classical Books and the Rituals of the State religion, but as a designation of *deified Heaven*, the great protecting god of China. To some it has been a matter of surprise that the Japanese, though they have so long introduced the ethical system of Confucius and its nomenclature, yet have never used the name Shangti. The reason of their so doing appears very obvious to me. The Japanese have their own system of nature worship. The sun is the great goddess of Japan. She is the progenitrix of their race of Emperors and the Protectress of their land. They never introduced the worship of Heaven as a god—and hence they had no occasion to use Shangti, which is a designation of deified Heaven.

I translate this designation 上帝, "The Ruler *above*," because all *uses* of the word and the *relations* of the ideas call for that meaning. In connection with the two great gods of the Chinese, Heaven and Earth their *relative* position is constantly referred to by the words "*above*" and "*below*" 上, 下. It is one of the most common phrases among the people "above is Heaven," and "below is Earth," 上有天, 下有地. among the words used as synonyms of "the Ruler above" as have "the Heaven azure," 上天, the "azure above" 上蒼 "the high canopy" 高穹 I suppose no one would insist on translating these, as, "The supreme Heaven," "The supreme azure," "The supreme canopy," yet they all refer to the one same object, deified Heaven. So we have "Heaven above and the people below," 上天下民. No one I suppose would think this should be translated "Supreme Heaven, and lowest people."

So in my opinion, Shangti is simply the Ruler *above*, to indicate its *relative* position to the earth god. Besides all this, there is not one expression in the whole of the Chinese Books to indicate any superiority of Heaven over the Earth. But they are frequently said *to be equal*—they are honored with the same worship and sacrifices, and their merit i said to be the same. If it is asked if the use of "above" is only to distinguish the relative positions of the gods, why do they not use the corresponding prefix to Earth. The reason appears to me obvious. As men, who are the writers, are all on the same plane or level with Earth as to locality, there would be no propriety in prefixing the corresponding prefix *below* to Earth. Heaven is *above* men and the Earth as to locality, hence there is great propriety in prefixing the word Shang before the object above, whether it is called Heaven, as Heaven above, or Ruler, as Ruler above. The fact that Ti 帝 Ruler, without the prefix Shang 上, is so very frequently used in the classics, and in the rituals, as the synonym of Heaven, and to designate it as the Ruler, shows that there is no special significance in the prefix Shang 上.

I come now to present the authority of Foreigners, who have used the Chinese language or translated from Chinese, as to the meaning of this phrase, Hwang T'ien Shangti. The Catholic missionary, P. Lacharme, who translated the Shiking into Latin, and which translation was edited by Julius Mohl, in 1830, translated Shangti, in the corresponding phrase "haou t'ien Shangti 昊天上帝, as in apposition with haou t'ien as stated by Dr. Legge, in his Shi-king, p. 530. P. Lacharme's translation reads in Latin, "Augustum coelum, qui est summus rerum dominus et dominator." The Catholic missionary, who translated the prayer of the Emperor K'ang Hi, which he offered at the time he sacrificed to Heaven when he was going forth to war against the Kaldan, translates Shangti in opposition with hwang t'ien thus. "Oh Sovereign Heaven, Supreme Emperor 皇天上帝! I invoke your aid with respectful confidence in the war that I am just now compelled to undertake. You have overwhelmed me with favors, you have shown me signal and extraordinary protection." See Huc's "Christianty in China, vol. III, p. 214; where he quoted from De Mailla, Hist. Gen de la China, Vol. II, p. 187. If Deified Heaven was not the object to which prayer was offered in such imperial sacrifices, then in case the words Shangti, which are here translated as in apposition with hwang t'ien, were omitted and only hwang t'ien remained, it would be hard to say what would be the meaning of the sentences. In Williams' "Middle Kingdom," there is a translation given of a prayer for rain, which was offered by the Emperor Taou Kwang in the year 1832, in a time of drought. In this very remarkable paper, the expression "hwang t'ien" 皇天 occurs *four times* in the form of *direct* address, *without* the words Shangti added to it. As thus: "Oh! alas, Imperial Heaven, 皇天, were not the world afflicted by extraordinary changes I would not dare to offer extraordinary services." "Prostrate, I beg Imperial Heaven (hwang t'ien) to pardon my iniquity." "Oh alas! Imperial Heaven, observe these things. Oh! alas! Imperial Heaven, be gracious to them." See Mid. Kingdom, Vol. I, pp. 369-371.

In the controversy which lasted among the Catholic missionaries, during the whole of the seventeenth century, in regard to what was called "The rites," there appears to have been no difference of opinion among the missionaries on this one point, as *to what*, prayer and sacrifice were offered by the Emperor at the winter solstice. All agreed that the sacrifice *was to Heaven* (T'ien). The point of the controversy among them was whether *deified Heaven* was worshipped, or whether Heaven was worshipped *as a symbol* merely of the Lord and Ruler of Heaven. That this was the point in discussion appears from the memorial, or petition, which some of the missionaries presented to the Emperor K'ang Hi, in the year 1699.—In that memorial, the memorialists say: "We believe that the sacrifices *offered to heaven* are not tendered to the visible heavens, which are seen above us, but to the supreme Master, Author, and Preserver of heaven and earth and all they contain." See Williams, Mid. King. vol. II. p. 309. This point is equally clear from the reply of the Emperor to the petition in which he said "T'ien means the true God." idem 309. If the translation accepted of the phrase "Hwang T'ien Shangti" had then been "The supreme Ruler of the Imperial Heaven, the controversy would not have been about T'ien, Heaven, but about Shangti. It would not have been said, as the memorialists say: "We believe the sacrifices *offered to Heaven;*" but they would have said "We believe the sacrifices offered to the Supreme Ruler of the Imperial Heavens." &c. It is perfectly clear that the only translation known to them, was that which is given by P. Lacharme, the translator, and K'ang Hi, as given above, "Imperial Heaven, Supreme Emperor," making "Shangti" *in apposition* with Imperial Heaven.

As the long continued discussion of "The rites" by the Catholic missionaries, has an intimate and important connection with the question what is the object which is worshipped by the Chinese, it is important to briefly refer to that discussion. My principle authority in regard to it, is "Christianity in China, &c.," by M. L'Abbé Huc, London 1857—the 2nd and 3 vols. Father Ricci reached Peking, the Capital of China, in 1590—and engaged in making himself useful to the government, in order to secure a permanent foot-hold. He was under a great temptation to look very leniently on the rites of the Chinese in worshipping Confucius, deceased parents, and Heaven. The two former were considered to be merely civil ceremonies, of no religious import, and the offerings to Heaven were explained as offerings to the Lord of Heaven. M. Huc says: 'It was a system which offered every facility to the missionaries, and that greatly assisted them in propagating Christianity. The ancient and only religion of the Chinese, had been confined to the worship of Heaven, (T'ien), of the wise men and of their ancestors.' Christianity, in China, Vol. II. p. 228. When Ricci died in 1610, he entrusted the care of the missions to Father Lombard, as the best qualified to take the charge of so important a trust. P. Lombard had, hitherto, out of respect to Ricci, suspended his judgment on the question of the rites. When the responsibility of the mission rested upon him, he studied and wrote upon the subject. He came to the conclusion "that the Chinese in reality recognized no divinity but Heaven" p. 229. "The use of the words, T'ien, and "Shangti, even, by which they designated *the divinity* were interdicted," p. 230. Thus the parties divided; those who sought worldly influence and power at Peking, were in favor of Ricci's views of the rites; the more spiritual and self-sacrificing laborers, whether they were Jesuits, Franciscans, vicar apostolic Dominicans, or were connected with the seminary of Foreign missions in Paris, held with P. Lombard. Some of the most distinguished and learned of those who held with P. Lombard, were Father Morales, a Dominican, Father Navarette, also a Dominican, M. Maigrot, Doctor of the Sorbonne, and vicar apostolic of Fuh Kien, P. Visdelom and many others, who were known as devoted and laborious missionaries.

Many of those who refused to accept the rites as allowable, were called to endure persecution for their opinions; whilst many of those who did accept them, were promoted to high honors. Bishop Maigrot, at the request or command of K'ang Hi, "cited from the Sacred Books of China fifty texts in support of his opinion that the rites were idolatrous." p. 266. If any copy of this compilation is extant, it would be of great importance in this inquiry. The Emperor, having all along coincided in the view that these rites were not idolatrous, was very angry that M. Maigrot furnished such strong proofs from the classics that the Emperor's opinion was not in accord with the teachings of the classics. It would appear that he never could forgive him. One statement of the nature of the first decisions of the Pope in regard to the non-idolatrous nature of the rites, reveals to us the nature of some of the arguments which were urged in favor of that opinion. "They obtained a third decree, which maintained the validity of the two former ones (one of which was in favor and one against the rites) by declaring that the Chinese ceremonies were forbidden to those *who thought them idolatrous*, and allowed to such as *regarded them as merely civil acts*." Here was where the mental reserve of the Jesuits came in. But nothing so effectually sets forth the utter incorrectness of the views of those who regarded the rites as not idolatrous as the language of the memorialists to the Emperor, K'ang Hi. They say: "We have always supposed that Confucius was honored in China as a legislator, and that it was in *this character alone* and *with this view solely*, that the ceremonies established in his honor were practiced. We believe that the ancestral rites are *only* observed in order to exhibit the love felt for them, and to hallow the remembrance of the good received from them during their life."*

We believe that the sacrifices offered to heaven, are not tendered to the visible heavens, which are seen above us, but to the supreme Master, Author, and Preserver of Heaven and Earth and all that they contain." Williams, Mid. King. Vol. II. pp. 309-10. All these different rites to Confucius, to ancestors, and to Heaven consisted of sacrifices and offerings, bowings down before them with prayers to each of the objects for protection and blessings. With the words of Jehovah, as expressed in the second commandment before us, "Thou shalt not make unto thee any

---

* To show the nature of the prayers offered to ancestors I present an example of one which was offered on the 12th year of Taou Kwang and the 1st day of the 3rd month. " I, Liu Kwang, the second son of the third generation presume to come before the grave of my ancestor Lin Kung. Revolving years have brought again the season of spring. Cherishing sentiments of veneration, I look up and sweep your tomb. Prostrate, I pray that you will come and be present; *that you will grant to your posterity that they may be prosperous and illustrious*; at this season of genial showers and gentle breezes, *I desire to recompense the root my existence*, and exert myself sincerely. Always *grant your safe protection. My trust is in your divine spirit.* Reverently I present the five-fold sacrifice of a pig, a fowl, a duck, a goose and a fish; also an offering of five plates of fruit, with oblations of spirituous liquors; earnestly entreating that you will come and view them, with most attentive respect this announciation is presented on high." Chi. Rep. vol. I, p. 202.

graven image, or any likeness of any thing that is in Heaven above, or that is in the earth beneath, or that is in the water under the earth: thou shall not bow down thyself to them, nor serve them," every Christian man and Biblical student must regard them all as forbidden by the command of Jehovah. If such services and prayers, offered to deceased men and to an object of nature, are not idolatrous services, there is no idolatry in the world.

Therefore, as the *facts* in regard to the worship of Heaven, the grammatical *construction* of the sentence, and the *weight* of *authority* both Chinese and Foreign, support the translation, which has been given of the phrase under consideration, viz., hwang T'ien Shangti, "Imperial Heaven, the Ruler above," I consider it as the true and correct translation, and hence it appears, that Shangti is the designation of deified Heaven, in reference to its being the Ruler over all things.

As reference has been made to the controversy, which existed, during the whole of the seventeenth century, on the question of the Chinese rites, among the Catholic Missionaries of that time, it will be interesting to note the result, to which, after long investigation, the Pope and his advisers arrived, on the whole matter. The main points of the decision are expressed, as follows: "Such practices being imbued with superstition, Christians must not be allowed to perform any ceremonies in the temples of Confucius, or offer oblations, such as are offered in his honor, every month, at the new and full moon.* * That, moreover, it must not be permitted Christians to make the less solemn oblations to their ancestors in temples or buildings dedicated to them, nor to serve or minister at such oblations *in any manner whatever;* Nor to render them any worship, or perform any ceremonies to their honor. That Christians must be forbidden to practice this worship, or these oblations or ceremonies, in the presence of the small tablets of ancestors in private houses, or at their tombs, or before interring the dead in the manner that is customary, either separately or conjointly with pagans, or to serve, minister or assist at them in any manner whatever.* * That to express our idea of the most high and good God, the name 'T'ien' and 'Shangti.' must *be absolutely rejected.* That for this reason it must not be permitted that tablets bearing the Chinese inscription 'King T'ien' 'adore Heaven' should be placed in Christian churches." Huc's Christianity in China, Vol. III. p. 410–411.

This, decision forbidding the use of both Heaven and Shangti in speaking of Jehovah, clearly implies that the See of Rome had, after full consideration, arrived at the conclusion, that as T'ien and Shangti were the names by which the chief god of the Chinese government, viz: deified Heaven, was commonly designated, they could not be used in speaking of Jehovah without danger of confounding him with the false god; and therefore, the Pope forbade their use entirely. There is a very singular use of the phrase "King-t'ien" by the emperors of China, which fully warrants the special prohibition of this phrase. Not only is it frequently used by the Emperors in edicts and prayers when speaking of their reverence for their great protector, but in the most solemn imperial announcements or statements, it is used somewhat in the same way as in the language of Western Rulers the phrase "by the grace of God, Emperor, &c," is used. In the last solemn Testament of Kang Hi he commences it thus 敬天承運皇帝制曰. "I, the Emperor, who honor Heaven and have received the throne by its order, say." This decision of the Roman See as to the rites in China, caused the missionaries to lose, in a great measure, the favor of Kang Hi, and their influence at the court of Peking; it caused a great many of those, who, during the continuance of the temporizing course in regard to the rites, had become adherents of Christianity, to withdraw from the connection, and the Catholic church has never since, had such a number of professed followers in China, as it had previous to that decision. But notwithstanding these apparently disastrous results of the decision of the Pope, every one who prefers truth and righteousness to mere temporary and outward success, must unite in approving of the decision, and in giving honor to Clement XI, who had the moral courage to give and to execute so righteous a decision, and one of such great importance to Christianity.

As the decision on the points referred to above, is in *such entire accord with the plain teachings of the Bible*, it ought to be widely made known to all the propagators of Christianity in this empire, and to all those who accept of its doctrines from among this people. And the decision ought to be *faithfully accepted* by all missionaries whether Catholic or Protestant.

I ought perhaps to refer to the fact, that there are some sinologists, who have given a different translation of this important phrase, which has been under consideration, lest some should suppose I am not aware of the fact. I am fully aware that one learned sinologist has published in a book, that the Emperor of China, when he goes to the altar of Heaven, worships "the supreme Ruler of the universe." It is well known that the ancient Chinese, from whom this worship has come down, supposed that the earth was an expanded surface surrounded by four seas: that the Heavens overshadowed this extended surface, and that there were, in this "overhanging canopy," the Sun, Moon and Stars, but having very little idea as to what they were. That was the *universe* to them. How inadequate a conception is *that* to what is suggested to our minds by the word *universe*, a word which naturally fills our minds with awe and adoration, in the conception of the vast system of worlds, and the systems of suns and of other worlds which are supposed to fill the *boundless immensity*. And what a glorious conception of the power and glory of the Great God does the idea of the universe give to us, for He "created the Heavens and all the hosts thereof." How inconsiderate it is to use an expression which recalls to us this grand and glorious idea, in reference to the worship of a heathen Emperor at the altar of deified Heaven.

I am also fully aware that the distinguished scholar and learned professor, Dr. Legge, has translated this phrase, "The supreme Ruler [dwelling] in the sovereign heavens." Notions of the Chinese, p. 25. I can only express my deep regret and great surprise, that so great a scholar should have fallen into so great an error in the translation of so important a phrase. I have examined his writings, and his translations of the Shoo-king and She-king, and I have failed to discover any satisfactory statement either of the facts of the case, or the grammatical construction on which he justifies his translation. He, in the main, disregards the opinions of Chinese commentators on that point, and also that of other sinologists. In the She-king at p. 530, where he controverts the translation of P. Lacharme, who translates Shangti as in apposition with Haou T'ien," he says: "Lacharme makes the two parts of the line in apposition.' 'Augustum coelum qui est summus rerum dominus et dominator.' But such an apposition of the personal name, and the vague designation of Heaven, especially with the epithet of great attached, is to my mind exceedingly *unnatural*." Dr. Legge's translation of the passage there is, "God [from his] great Heaven."

Dr. Legge well knows that all idolatry is "unnatural" and unreasonable. If the supposition was, that it was the great Heaven, the material Heaven as a part of dead and inert matter that was meant, it would be *unnatural* and *incongruous* to the last degree. But that is not the idea of the Heathen Chinese. Dr. Legge, in the Shoo King at p. 283, on the passage "Heaven and Earth is the Parent of all creatures," says: "There can be no doubt that *the deification of* Heaven and Earth, which appears in the text, took its rise from the Yih King, of which King Wan may properly be regarded as the author." What is involved in the "deification of Heaven?" It clearly implies, that Heaven is regarded *as a god*, and as such, he is considered to possess life, volition, power, and all the attributes that belong to the conception of the supreme Ruler. When *Heaven is thus conceived* of by them as a god, possessed of all the attributes which Dr. Legge says are ascribed to Shangti, the considering of Heaven as in apposition with Shangti *is very congruous*. The ascribing of these attributes to an object of nature, is *very unnatural* to us, enlightened as we are by the Bible. But that is just what the Bible and the history of all nations show to us that mankind in every age and country has done. The Egyptians, Syrians, Hindoos and Grecians were just as enlightened as the Chinese of the same age were. And when it is so universally admitted that the people of these nations deified the objects of nature, *why* is it regarded as so incredible that the Chinese, from the earliest times, have deified Heaven, and that they continue to do so to this time? When it is *admitted* that the Chinese regarded Heaven as a god, and clothed him with the attributes of the great God to a wonderful extent, there is nothing unnatural or incongruous in putting Shangti in apposition with Heaven, as Lacharme has done, in the passage under consideration. His Latin will read thus in English "great *Heaven*, who is the highest Lord and Ruler of things." If Dr. Legge will, in his very admirable translations of the Shoo-king and She-king, give T'ien the sense of Heaven, as a god, as the great god, and to Shangti the sense of Ruler or Ruler above, as the synonym of Heaven, then there will be little else to be desired in regard to the translation of these books. But in view of the full proof which I have given, that deified Heaven is the great god and protector of the Chinese, and that Shangti is a designation of this false god,—I can not for a moment say with Dr. Legge—"this god is our God." I hold on the contrary that he is one of the gods "which shall perish." But our God is Jehovah, "Who of old hast laid the foundations of the Earth ; and the heavens are the works of thine hands. They shall perish, but thou shalt endure ; yea, all of them shall wax old like a garment ; as a vesture shalt thou change them, and they shall be changed ; but thou art the same, and thy years shall have no end." Ps. 102: 25-27. And long before the destruction of the visible heavens this worshipping of Heaven shall cease ; for the knowledge of God, Jehovah, shall fill the whole Earth.

In connection with this worship of Heaven, Earth and men, by the Chinese there is a passage in the prophet Isaiah, which has new force and application as covering the whole ground and cutting away all the roots of these various idolatries. "Thus saith God Jehovah, he that created the heavens, and stretched them out ; he that spread forth the Earth and that which cometh out of it ; he that giveth breath unto the people upon it, and spirit unto them that walk therein : I Jehovah have called thee in righteousness and will hold thine hand and will keep thee and give thee for a covenant to the people, for a light to the Gentiles. Is. 42: 5-6. Thus Jehovah is the Creator and Lord of all the things of which the nations have made gods unto themselves.

There are some things which present themselves for consideration in connection with the results which have been arrived at in these inquiries, which may be adverted to.

1st.—These discussions have brought to view a great system of idolatry which has hitherto received but little attention from the missionaries. It is more deeply rooted in the hearts of the people than any other, because it is the indigenous system, and because it is sanctioned by all the sages of antiquity : it is also more securely entrenched, because it is the state religion, and it has all the prestige which the support of the government can give to it. Against this great system of the early worship in China we will need to unite all our forces, and to cooperate with all harmony of purpose and aim, in order to effect its overthrow. We must explain to all the true nature of idolatry, whether it exists in high or low places ; but with all charity and love for those who are engaged in its practice. There must be no excusing, or covering it over with glosses or excuses, as if it was not sin against the great Lord of all nations, Jehovah.

2nd.—The proof which has been presented, that Shangti is the distinctive designation of an individual Being, deified Heaven, and which Being is the great protecting god of this Empire and people, makes it necessary that a most careful consideration of the use of this word be made by those who have hitherto used Shangti as the standard designation of the true God. Most of those who have so used it, have used it for that purpose, under the impression, that it was *not in any way connected with idolatry.* Hitherto it has been conceded that Yuh Whang Shangti is an idol. And also that when Shangti is applied to the Northern Emperor, Peh Ti, it designates an idol. It has been contended that Shangti of the classics is free from all connection with idolatry. But it has *now* been shown that Shangti of the classics is not only not the same as Jehovah, but that it is the designation of deified Heaven and therefore it is the designation of a false god. Hence now it must be admitted that Shangti of the classics is also a false god. This fact now gives rise to the practical question, can the name or designation of a well *known* and *universally recognized false god,* be properly used to designate the true God? I am satisfied that all the missionaries will now give this question the most prayerful and careful consideration. I pray God, that they all may be guided to a right conclusion. I feel assured that my brethren will suffer from me a few remarks on this point, which I make in no spirit of controversy, but simply to further the intersts of truth, which is the end *that we all seek,* though we do not always see alike as to what is truth. In my former article at page 78 of the *Chinese Recorder* for 1877, I, in remarking on "shin," that though it has the meaning of spirit as well as god, said that if used for spirit, when speaking of *those* that are worshipped, as for instance the Holy Spirit, there was great danger of its being understood in such connection in the sense of God. I there say, "So in the deification of God as given in the Gospel by St. John, in Chap. 4: 24. 'God is a Spirit;' if this is expressed in Chinese "Shangti Nai Shin," there is great danger, that from the association of ideas with the usage of Shin in such connection for god, it will be understood as saying that Shangti is a god; which is of course true, but it is not the idea there expressed." According to a statement published in the *Recorder* for 1877, page 259—this very text was presented to the assistants at Foochow as a Thesis for essays—and a great majority of the writers understood the text to mean that Shangti is a god, thus more than justifying the fear that I had expressed in regard to that point. It is my strong conviction, that if any suitable plan could be devised, to arrive at the understanding which the members of the native churches have in regard to Shangti, in the districts where Shangti is used for God in preaching the Gospel among this people, it would be found, that a large majority of the members have the idea that the *native Idol,* which is commonly designated by that name in the said district, is referred to. This must be the case in the very nature of things, and by the laws of the human mind. The people have been accustomed from their childhood to hear the idol Yuh hwang called Shangti. When they hear the word Shangti, they necessarily think of Yuh hwang, and nothing else. All our ideas of things would be *confused*, if we did not thus associate the *same Being* with the *name* of that *Being* when we heard it spoken. I *cannot* consider that Jupiter is spoken of when I hear the name Jehovah, because Jehovah and Jupiter in my mind are two *distinct Beings* and I always think of each respective Being when I hear each name. A Chinese who all his life has heard the Idol Yuh hwang called Shangti must always think of Yuh hwang when he hears the name Shangti. He cannot understand that a new and different Being is referred to when he hears the familiar sound Shangti. For a while, when under direct instruction on *that point*, he may answer, that by Shangti, Jehovah is referred to. But when away from the instruction, the law of association and long established thought will come back, and *Shangti to him means Yuh whang*. Some will get the idea that Jehovah is the *same as Shangti*, and that is the reason why he is called Shangti. By reason of the laws of the human mind which lead us to connect or associate the same person or Being with the name by which we have always heard that person or Being called, I express the opinion, that a large number of the church members where Shangti is used for God, understand, by Shangti, the native Idol which is commonly designated by that name in that region. I have no means of verifying my opinion. But as the other opinion has been verified by a very unexpected incident, I expect to see this opinion, sooner or later, shown to be correct in some way. While writing, an incident has come to my knowledge to this effect. A missionary was surrounded by a group of people telling them of the Gospel and of Jesus, using Shangti when speaking of God. One of the most intelligent of the native Christians of that neighbourhood, was standing in the company. He volunteered a side remark to the crowd to help them to understand the Foreigner. His remark was to the effect that " Shangti means Yuh hwang." Here is an instance of a church member, who, while *listening* to the remarks of the missionary, having this association of the name of the native Idol so strong in his mind, that he tells the heathen hearers that the missionary means Yuh hwang. So far when Shangti is used for God in preaching.

3rd.—I come now to say a few words when Shangti is used in the Sacred Scriptures as the translation of Elohim. I now speak of it as used in the sense of Shangti of the classics. I suppose a literary Chinese takes up a copy of the Bible, and he reads in the first chapter of Genesis, "In the beginning Shangti created the Heavens and the Earth." What does he understand by this declaration?—He having read the classics knows that Shangti is the designation of a god of great power and rule. He at once concludes that it was *this Being*, whom he has long known of by the name of Shangti, that created the world. If Dr. Legge's opinion, that the *Shangti* of the classics is the *same Being as Jehovah* is correct, then the *Chinese reader* gets the correct idea, for the Bible *means* to teach that the God Jehovah created the heavens and the earth. But if that opinion *is not correct*, and it is the correct opinion that Shangti is the designation of deified Heaven, then what is the meaning that the Chinese reader gets? Why, it is that Shangti, which is the same as deified Heaven, created the Heavens and the Earth—and you *cannot change* that idea. The Chinese scholar *knows* that Shangti means that particular Being and nothing else. And this passage is thus made to teach that another, and a different Being from Jehovah, created the Heavens and the Earth.

Let us consider another passage of the Sacred Scriptures in which Shangti occurs as the translation of Elohim. The first commandment reads, " I am Jehovah, thy Shangti.* * Thou shalt have no other Shangti before me." Ex. 20; 2, 3. We are all agreed as to what the original means, and as to what it is intended to express in Chinese. In this passage Jehovah claims to be the God of all men, of every nation, and forbids all men, as well as each individual man, to have any other God beside Jehovah. The present inquiry is to find out what the Chinese will understand from the translation into Chinese where Shangti is used to translate Elohim. It is admitted that this Shangti is the Shangti of the Chinese classics. The Shangti of the classics is the special protector of the Chinese Empire and people. He appoints the Emperor, so that he is called in reference to being so appointed, "the son of Heaven." (Heaven being the same Being with Shangti and the synonym of Shangti.) Shangti changes the dynasty when, by wickedness or misruling, the existing dynasty has forfeited his favor. Shangti is prayed to for fruitful seasons, and when, for the sins of the people or of the rulers, he sends drought or other calamities, he is sought unto for deliverance from the calamity. Thanks are given to Shangti for the fruits of the Earth, for victories in time of battle, &c. The Chinese government and people have thus for 4,000 years recognized Shangti as *the protector* and Ruler of this country. When therefore a revelation comes to them from a Divine Being, as it does in the Bible, and says to this people, "I am Jehovah, thy Shangti," it appears to me beyond all doubt, that they can only understand, that it is the Shangti whom they have so long known and worshipped that speaks to them. They know no other *Being* who is called Shangti. And when a Divine Being thus speaks to them and styles himself "thy Shangti," who can they suppose is speaking to them, but *the* Shangti they have so long worshipped? If Dr. Legge's opinion, that Shangti is the *same* Being as Jehovah, is correct, then Jehovah is, of course, the Shangti of this people and thus the translation *is most apposite and correct*, for that is what the passage expressly says. "I am Jehovah thy Shangti;" and this declaration would be *particularly true* and *appropriately said* of the Chinese people; just as *distinctively true of them*, as it was of the Israelites, the chosen people of God. But if the opinion of Dr. Legge *is not true,* (and it has been *abundantly proven* that it is not true,) and if it is true, that Shangti is the designation of deified Heaven, which is the great divinity of the Chinese government, then what follows? In my opinion, it necessarily gives to the Chinese reader the idea that Jehovah is the same as the Shangti which they have so long worshipped; and that they shall worship no other Shangti but him, for they cannot suppose that the name of their Shangti was given to another Being. I do not for a moment intimate that any, with this understanding of its meaning, have preferred this term to translate Elohim. I only ask my brethren to consider what is the meaning which the use of Shangti to translate Elohim, gives the Sacred Scriptures. Dr. Legge in his translation of the Shoo-king and She-king, has made it clear *beyond all doubt,* that Shangti is the *distinctive title of an individual Being,* which has been worshipped by the Chinese from the earliest period of their history; and that Heaven is everywhere interchanged with Shangti, as referring to the same Being. I have shown that that Being is deified Heaven. Hence Shangti *can no longer* be considered *in any sense,* as a common noun which might be applied to any worshipped Being. When the words Shang-ti are used they can properly only be understood to refer to that Being, to which that designation has always been given in the Chinese classics. There is now therefore no middle ground. Shangti is either the same Being as Jehovah as Dr. Legge maintains, or Shangti is the designation of deified Heaven, to which the Chinese *have given the glory which belongs to Jehovah.* Hence, when Shangti is used, it conveys to the Chinese reader *necessarily* the idea of that distictive and individual Being—just as much as the title "The emperor Napoleon" suggests the idea of the one man, who was the conqueror of so many nations of Europe. Therefore, when a Chinese reads the verse, "Shangti created the Heavens and the Earth"—it can only mean that the Being, who is designated Shangti, created the Heaven and the Earth—and hence the transcendent importance of the question which has occupied so much time in its discussion, viz; What Being is designated by the words Shangti? So far as I know it has never been considered proper to choose the designation of an individual false god and apply it to Jehovah. It would not appear best for us in China to depart from a rule, which has been observed by the propagators of Christianity during all the past period of its dissemination among so many nations.

I see no other safe course to pursue in the matter except the *common* and *general use* of the divinely revealed name of the one true God, Jehovah, to designate the God we seek to make known to this people, and in connection with this peculiar and proper name of the true God, use such others words and phrases as may be deemed most suitable to express His various attributes and relations.

4th.—I have not referred to the fact that the Chinese have, from the earliest period of their history, worshipped other objects conjointly with Heaven, as an argument to show that by Heaven, the great God cannot be intended. But every one must acknowledge that the fact that the earth, the Imperial ancestors, and the gods of the land and the grain, have been always worshipped conjointly with Heaven, precludes the idea that by Heaven, the true God, Jehovah, can be understood. It has been repeatedly stated, that the use of Heaven to designate God in the Parable of the Prodigal son by our Blessed Lord sanctions the use of Heaven as referring to God. His language does most certainly sanction the use of the word Heaven as a symbol of the God of Heaven. But in the mind of our Lord and Saviour, in the passage referred to, and in the minds of Christians when using the same language, *the great God* is the Being who is referred to, and heaven, which is the work of his hand, is but the symbol of its great Lord and Creator. But in all the Chinese Books, *Heaven*, deified Heaven, is the positive Being spoken of, and Shangti is the designation of Heaven as the Ruler above. Hence the use of the word Heaven in the Sacred Scriptures by our Lord, is *as different as possible from* the manner of using Heaven in the Chinese classics.

5th.—I think it quite proper to refer to some sentences which I have met with on these investigations, which show the use of "*Shin*" in the ritual and the classics. In the ritual of the sacrifice to Heaven, "Shin" is used in these different senses. In one place it is said. "The head of the Board of Rites shall then direct some officers of the Sacrificial court to enter the "Circular Hall of the Imperial Expanse" and reverently invite the tablets of the gods out." In this place "Shin" designates *both Heaven and ancestors*. The Emperor had just previously entered that Hall and "offered incense before the tablets of the Ruler above and the respective Holy ones." Now they are collectively invited to come out. This manifests most clearly *the equality* with which Heaven and the ancestors are regarded. Their tablets are kept on the same depository, and they are invited to come out at the same time. I have met with this sentence, stating a usage that prevailed in the Sung Dynasty. "First they [the emperors] sacrificed to the ancestors and then sacrificed to Heaven and Earth.¹"

In the ritual where the shrine of Heaven is specially referred to three times, it is designated the shrine of *Ti Shin* 帝神, which I have translated the Ruler-god. I have so done in accordance with a usage of of this language, as stated by P. Premare in his "Notitia Linguæ Sinicæ," page 155, par. 4th; where he says, "Shi jin 詩人 is an' ode man, Wăn jin 文人 is a writer of essays and Tsui jin 罪人 is one who sins"—as, an ode man is one who makes odes, an essay man is one who writes essays and a sin man is one who commits sin, so by the same usage Ti shin 帝神 is a god who rules. But in "the ritual for prayer to Hea-

---

¹ 宋室之禮. 先享宗廟, 乃祀天地, (經世文編).

ven on any special occasion" there is a very important use of "shin." The only tablet that is present on that occasion is that of Heaven with the full title 皇天上帝神位 "the god, imperial Heaven, Ruler above's tablet." In speaking of receiving this tablet, and in sending it away it is called "Shin," *simply*, the god. I have also met with a precisely similar use of "shin" in a memorial addressed to an Emperor of the Han Chin in which the memorialist is asking* "that the title of Earth should be changed from Sovereign Earth 后土 to 皇地后祇 imperial Earth Sovereign Producer, because the god (*i. e.* Heaven) had been called 皇天上帝 for a long time.[1]"

The original and normal use of "shin" is in connection with deified Heaven, as it is called 天神 the Heaven god; just as Ki is the word uses in connection with deified Earth 地祇. It must be particularly observed that T'ien shin 天神 and 地祇 Ti ki have two well defined used. Such uses are authoritatively indicated in the ritual. One use is when they distinctively indicate Heaven and Earth respectively. Then each expression is singular, and it is placed in the highest place in the column, which shows clearly that Heaven and Earth are meant. When T'ien shin is used to designate the deified sun, moon and stars. and the deified powers of nature, as the winds, the clouds, the rain and the thunder, then the expression is plural, and it is printed in the second place in the column to indicate that they are secondary objects of worship. The same thing is true of Ti ki 地祇, when it refers to the deified mountains and hills, the seas and the streams, it is plural, and in the ritual it is placed in the second place in the column of characters to indicate that it refers to objects of secondary worship. This "usus loquendi" in reference to these two expressions, prevails all through the classics. Sometimes it is most difficult to distinguish which is the true meaning, for it is not always possible to say certainly, whether Heaven itself and Earth itself are referred to or not—and we have not anything to guide us there, as we have in the ritual. In it, the position the character occupies in the column, manifests the meaning beyond all doubt. I now present some passages from the classics in which "shin" is used interchangeably with Heaven. The Emperor of the Wei Chin named Ming Ti says: "I, in my teaching have done something displeasing to the imperial *god*, therefore *Heaven* above has sent something to awaken me from my indifference." Siau Yung sz in explaining sacrifices, says; "The great ceremony is the sacrifice to *Heaven*

---

[1] 又泰, 舊神稱皇天上帝太一, 兆曰泰時, 地祇曰后土, 今宜地祇稱皇地后祇, 兆曰廣時, (王莽奏議見杜佑通典).

* From this statement it would appear that Heaven had the title "imperial" as early as the Han Dynasty which occupied the throne from 202 B. C. to A. D. 221; and because Heaven had this title the memorialist proposes that it should be given to Earth also. The use of this title would appear to have fallen into disuse ; and according to the collected statutes of the Ming Dynasty it was restored to Heaven with great ceremony in 1535.

and Earth: therefore the Chow Li, to honor and distinguish it,[1] says: 'Sacrifice to the great god and the great Producer.'"[2] In the chapter on music, in Li ki, it is said, "When the ceremonies and music of the ancient kings were agreeable to the disposition of Heaven and Earth, they were able to have communication with the virtue of *the god*' and of the Ming."[3] The word Ming is used as a synomym of Ki. And hence 神明 "Shin ming" is synonomous with 神祇 "Shin Ki." Chang Kiun says of an Emperor, that "When he was about to attend to Kian sacrifice, he had not yet sacrificed to the "*Shin*" or the Ki; and having obtained an animal made it a victim for sacrifice; because of this Heaven manifested that it received the sacrifice of Wu Ti 武帝.[4]

In the ode Chen-jang of the She, the writer again and again appeals to Heaven. And in one stanza, he has a parallelism using " shin " in the second line, for Heaven of the first. Thus "Why is it that *Heaven* reproves? Why is it that *the god* does not bless:"[5] And Chau Tsz writes " When *Heaven* and Earth are in harmony, all things are in accord; therefore *the god* and the producer are moved with delight."[6]

The sacrifice " will ascend to imperial *Heaven*, and *the god* above will receive[7] it." Here *Shin* refers to *Heaven*, the god above is of the same meaning as the Ruler above. If any one insists that Shangti should be translated "Supreme Ruler," then in this passage by the same usage " Shang shin " should be translated " Supreme god," meaning Heaven. Of sentences thus speaking of the worship of Earth, and its being equal to Heaven, showing Heaven and Shangti being used interchangeably, and " Shin " also being used in speaking of Heaven, and sentences in which the emperor recognises Heaven as father, and Earth as mother, &c., &c. I have more than three hundred and fifty.—But these are sufficient to show how these things are spoken of in the Chinese Books.

In this ritual there is another usage of "Shin" which it is important to notice. It is this, *the manner* in which it is written when it is applied to any of the objects of the great sacrifice and when it is applied to other objects of worship. When it is used in reference to Heaven, to Earth and the Imperial ancestors, "Shin" is then printed in the *highest place* in the column, on *a level* with Heaven, Shangti and Earth. But wherever in the ritual, it is used to refer to other objects of worship, it is then written in the second place in the column of characters. This usage is very similar to our use of the word God in the Bible. When

---

[1] 朕施化有不合於皇神，故上天有以窬之. （魏明帝日蝕不許禳祀詔.）
[2] 禮重祭天地，故周禮鄩而別之曰祀大神祇. （蕭穎士郊祀疏.）
[3] 禮樂順天地之情，達神明之德. （樂記.）
[4] 今郊祀未見於神祇，而獲獸以饋，此天之所以示饗也. （終軍白麟對.）
[5] 天何以刺，何神不富. （詩大雅瞻卬之篇.）
[6] 天地和則萬物順，故神祇恪. （周子通書.）
[7] 升聞皇天，上神歆焉. （鼓禮.）

it is used to designate Jehovah, the only true God, we print it with a capital G, but when it is used to refer to other objects of worship, then it is written gods, commencing with a small g to indicate that they are not the great God. The manner in which "Shin" is used in the Imperial ritual, appears to me, to fully *warrant* the use of "shin" in connection with the peculiar and distinctive name Jehovah, when speaking of the one true and the false gods. The need of *a word* to be used in these applications is admitted by all. It appears to me that the use of shin in this two-fold application not only meets the need, but that its use in such a two-fold application, is, so to speak, *authorized* and *sanctioned* by the manner in which it is used in the Imperial ritual of the sacrifices to Heaven and Earth. For in that ritual it has a two-fold application, one when applied to the chief gods and the other when applied to inferior gods.

It will be interesting to many readers to notice the analogies with Scripture teachings which are found in this the most ancient form of idolatry existing on the earth. The objects of worship are the T'ien shin, the Ti Ki and the Jin kwei. T'ien shin is stated by Kang Hi to be "The one who draws, or stretches out all things."[1] Jehovah says "Thus saith God Jehovah, he that created the heavens and *stretched them out*, he that spread forth the earth, and that which cometh out of it." Is. 42: 5. "He hath *stretched* out the Heaven by his understanding. Jer. 51: 15. To him that *stretched out* the earth above the waters. Ps. 136: 6. The Ti Ki is defined in K'ang Hi, "The one who produces all things."[2] It was stated above that "these all things" include "both animate and inanimate things." In Genesis we read—"And the *earth* brought forth grass, and herb yielding seed after its kind, and the tree yielding fruit, whose seed is in itself, after his kind." Gen. 1: 12. "And God said, let the *waters* bring forth abundantly the moving creature that hath life, and fowl that may fly above the earth on the open firmament of heaven." Gen. 1: 20. "And God said, let the *earth* bring forth the living creature after his kind, cattle and creeping thing, and beast of the earth after his kind ; and it was so." Gen 1: 24. "And the Lord God formed man of the dust of the ground." Gen. 2: 7. The third object of worship in this early worship of the Chinese is the Jin kwei. The word kwei is defined by K'ang Hi thus; "The Shuh wan says, "man *returned* to what he was is called Kwei or [manes]. The Book I Ya says "kwei, to explain it is *returned.* Lieh Tsze says, when the soul leaves the body, each *returns* to its original, therefore they are styled kwei—kwei is the same as *returned:* returned to their original state."[3] There is also a colloquial expression which says, "man was made of the dust, therefore when a man dies, he returns to the

---

[1] 天神,引出萬物者. (字典)
[2] 地祇,提出萬物者. (字典)
[3] 說文云. 人所歸爲鬼,爾雅云. 鬼之爲言歸也, 列子云, 精神離形各歸其眞,故謂之鬼, 鬼, 歸也, 歸其眞宅. (字典)

bosom of the earth and he is then at peace."¹ How strikingly these are in accord with the teachings of the Bible. "In the sweat of thy face shalt thou eat bread, till thou *return* unto the ground; for out of it wast thou taken, for dust thou art, and unto dust shalt thou return." Gen. 3: 19. "Then shall the dust return to the earth as it was, and the spirit shall return to God who gave it. Ecle. 12: 7. Thus while the word of God declares that the Heavens and the Earth were *created* by God, and that God caused all things to *proceed* from the earth, men in their vain imaginations have supposed that the power was in the inert matter. The supposition in regard to souls of the departed is nearly the same among the Chinese, as it was among the Romans, who called them "manes" which is defined by Andrews in his Latin-English Lexicon, "The deified souls of the *departed*.

I have now finished the discussion of these two points which, it appeared to me, needed elucidation. The arguments which are presented in the first part, appear to me to establish the fact beyond all doubt, that Shangti of the classics is not the same Being as Jehovah, though they are not all the arguments that might be presented. Since, in the second part, it is shown what object is designated Shangti, the first point admits of no further discussion. On the second point, the proofs have been much more abundant and conclusive than I could have supposed. Unless we can suppose that this people have been mistaken for these four thousand years, in regard to the object to which the sacrifices and worship have been offered by their Emperors, then that object is deified Heaven. The abundance and clearness of the evidence in proof of the fact, that the great god of the Chinese is deified Heaven has surprised me; and I suppose it will equally surprise most of my readers. I submit these evidences and proofs to their consideration. I did not comprehend the matter till since I entered upon these inquiries. To many of my readers the results will be equally new and surprising, as they have been to myself. My only desire is that the truth may prevail. I pray that God may guide us all into the truth in this matter, as well as into all truth. Asking the blessing of God to attend this discussion, which was commenced with the desire that His name might be glorified, I commend it to the candid consideration of all my readers and of my missionary brethren.

¹ 人是坭做的, 所以人死, 歸回土裡頭就安樂了. （諺語）

NOTE.—To many readers it will be interesting to read the translation of a passage from Homer's Iliad, which shows how very like the idolatry of Greece was to that of China—The passage is Book III of the Iliad, lines 276-78, at the time when Paris and Menelaus were to engage in single conflict and end the strife. Both parties called upon the god's to be witness to the engagement which was made to this effect—The invocation was thus made?

"O Father Jove! Who rulest from Ida height,
Most great! Most glorious! And *thou Sun*, who see'st
And hearest all things! *Rivers!* And thou *Earth!*
And ye, who after death beneath the Earth
Your vengeance wreak on souls of men forsworn,
Be witness ye, and this our covenant guard."
        Earl Derby's Translation. Vol. I. Page 69.

ERRATA.

Page 53, 1st line for "Opposition" read "Apposition."
,, ,, 22nd, ,, ,, "Overshading" ,, "Overshadowing."
,, ,, 27th ,, ,, "King of Heaven" ,, "King of Hea."
,, 54, 2nd ,, ,, "Rule" ,, "Ruler."
,, ,, 24 & 25th line for "as have 'the Heaven azure'" read "we have 'the Heaven above.'"
,, 56, 11th line for "P. Lacherme, the translator of Kanghi" read "P. Lacherme and the translator of Kanghi."
,, ,, 6th ,, omit "vicar apostolic."
,, ,, 17th ,, for "principle" read "principal."
,, 62, 29th ,, ,, "deification" ,, "definition."

NOTE.

In consequence of the error of the copyist there are some errors in the Chinese text. The error consists in the first character of many lines commencing at a wrong elevation. The elevation at which the character is placed indicates the rank of the Being whose name is thus placed—To correspond with the imperial text, the first character in each of the lines indicated, should be placed one place lower in the line, as compared with the other lines, than they now are: viz., on page 1 in the 1st, 2nd, 3rd, 4th and 5th lines; on p. 3: in every line; on p. 4: in the 1st, 2nd, 4th, 5th, 6th and last line; on p. 5. in the 1st to 7th, 10th and 11th lines; on p. 7: in the 3rd line, and on p. 17: in the 1st, 2nd, 3rd, 4th and 5th lines.

神位還御

皇祇室

皇帝出至北門外陞禮輿法駕鹵簿前導導迎樂作奏祐平之章

皇帝回鑾王公從各官以次退不陪祀王公百官仍朝服於

午門外跪迎

午門鳴鐘王公隨

駕入至內金水橋恭候

皇帝還宮各退〇因事祇告遣官將事太常寺設黃幄於

方澤太常卿率所屬恭請

方澤地祇神位安奉幄內太常贊禮郎引遣官入

方澤北門左門由外壝北左門入內壝北左門詣

方澤第二成子階下拜位上香奠獻均升自西階讀祝由第一成子階右降至第二成讀祝拜位

仍降西階復位餘儀均與

圜丘祇告同

皇地祇位前拱舉

　　司詣

皇地祇位前奉箋琮退送

神奏寧平之章

配位前帛饌香恭送燎所

皇帝率羣臣行三跪九拜禮有司奉祝次帛次饌次香恭送瘞坎奉

皇帝轉立拜位旁西嚮候祝帛過復位

從位香帛均由東西階奉送各瘞所樂作

配位帛燎半奏望瘞恭導

皇帝由內墻北右門出至望瘞位望瘞引分獻官各詣左右門外望瘞奏禮成恭導

皇帝由外壇北右門出入大次更衣禮部尚書率太常官恭請

皇帝詣飲福受胙拜位六侍衛二人進立於左奉福胙官降立於右

皇帝跪左右執事官咸跪右官進福酒

皇帝受爵拱舉授左官進胙受胙亦如之三拜與復位率羣臣行三跪九拜禮徹饌奏貞平之章有

壇詣

皇地祇位前司爵官跪進爵

皇帝跪獻爵奠正中興退就讀祝拜位立司祝至祝案前跪三叩奉祝版跪案左樂暫止

皇帝跪羣臣皆跪司祝讀祝畢奉祝版詣

皇地祇位前跪安於案三叩退樂作

皇帝率羣臣行三拜禮興詣

配位前以次獻爵儀同贊禮郎引分獻官出東西階升壇各詣

從位前上香奠帛以次獻爵畢降階退立原位樂止武功之舞退文舞八佾進行亞獻禮奏安平之

章舞羽籥之舞

皇帝陞

壇以次獻爵奠於左儀如初獻復位行終獻禮奏時平之章

皇帝陞

壇以次獻爵奠於右儀如亞獻復位分獻官獻爵均如初樂止文德之舞退太常官贊

賜福胙光祿卿二人就西案奉福胙進至

舞與亞獻同

皇帝上柱香次三上瓣香典

皇帝詣玉帛案前司玉帛官跪進篚

皇帝跪受篚奠玉帛典儀以次詣

列聖配位前上香奠帛儀同贊引官奏復位

皇帝復位廻進俎

皇帝轉立拜位旁西嚮有司貯燙於壺恭執自壇下陟子階升詣

皇地祇位

列聖位前各跪拱舉典以羹沃俎者三皆退由西階降

皇帝復位奏含平之章

皇帝陞

壇詣

皇地祇位

配位前跪進俎與復位行初獻禮司爵官各奉爵進奏太平之章舞干戚之舞

皇帝陞

凡陞壇行禮復位皆有奏後同

皇帝出大次盥洗贊引太常卿恭導

皇帝由外壝北右門入內壝北右門陞子階至二成黃幄次拜位前立太常贊禮郞引分獻官四人由北左門入至階前夾甬道立鴻臚官引陪祀王公位階下百官位外壝門外均就位左右序立均南嚮典儀官贊樂舞生登歌執事官各共迺職

奏就位

皇帝就拜位立迺瘞毛血迎

司樂官贊舉迎

神樂奏中平之章 凡舉樂皆司樂官唱贊後同

皇帝行三跪九拜禮王公百官均隨行禮司香官各奉香盤司玉帛官各奉篚進奏廣平之章贊引

贊引官奏跪拜興

官奏陞

壇恭導

皇帝詣第一成

皇地祇位前司香官跪進香贊引官奏跪

皇帝跪奏上香

以下自瘞毛血至徹職皆典儀官唱贊

武舞八佾進贊引官

從位遣分獻官上香行禮
皇帝詣
方澤視
壇位詣
神庫視籩豆詭視牲牢畢由內壝北右門出外壝北右門至神路左陞輦詣
齋宮陪祀王公百官咸采服分班集
齋宮門外恭候
皇帝入酒退祭日日出前七刻太常卿詣
齋宮告時
皇帝御祭服乘禮輿出降輿乘輦鑾儀衛校鳴
齋宮鐘
皇帝至外壝北門外神路左降輦贊引太常卿二人恭導入大次竢禮部尚書率太常官詣
皇祇室恭請
神位安奉黃幄畢太常卿奏請行禮

太和門階下巳刻太常卿詣

乾清門奏請

皇帝詣齋宮

皇帝御龍袍袞服乘禮輿出宮內大臣侍衛前引後扈如常儀至

太和門階下降輿乘輦

駕發警蹕

午門鳴鐘法駕鹵簿前導不陪祀王公文武各官咸朝服跪送導迎鼓吹設而不作鑾儀衛校鳴

齋宮鐘

皇帝入壇西門至

方澤北門外降輦贊引太常卿二人恭導

皇帝由右門入詣

皇祇室於

皇地祇

列聖前上香畢行三跪九拜禮

天柱

永寧三山次西嶽

四海在其次

五鎮

隆業

昌瑞二山東嶽

四瀆在其次均設黃幄

皇地祇黃琮一帛一犢一登一鉶二籩豆各十有二尊一爵一鑪一鐙四

列聖均帛一犢一登一鉶籩豆各二籩豆各十有二尊一爵三鑪一鐙四

從位各帛一每幄均牛一羊一豕一登一銅二籩簋各二籩豆各十尊一爵三琖三十鑪一鐙二玉

帛寶於篚牲載於俎尊實酒疏布羃勺具先祭一日樂部設中和韶樂於壇下分左右懸鑾儀

衛陳法駕鹵簿於

午門外金鐃於

永寧五陵山從祭

皇地祇位第一成北嚮

列聖東西嚮

四從位第二成

五嶽
五鎮
四海
四瀆
啓運

五嶽
啓運

天柱
隆業
昌瑞

欽定大清會典卷之三十八

礼部

　祠祭清吏司

　大祀二

　凡祭

地之禮兆陰位

北郊曰

方澤其制二成四周以方坎瀦水以夏日至祭

皇地祇奉

太祖高皇帝

太宗文皇帝

世祖章皇帝

聖祖仁皇帝

世宗憲皇帝配以

皇天上帝位

四從位陪祀王公以下咸兩冠素服三獻禮終樂闋列舞童十有六人為皇舞衣元衣韎韐靺歌
御製雲漢詩八章以祈優渥餘儀及樂章均與
常雩同雨則報祀遣官朝服行禮如常儀已齋未祈而雨報祀亦如之 謹
列聖家法念切民天偶遇亢暘輒先期竭誠祈請順治康熙年間皆嘗
特命禮臣議常雩大雩典禮以昭至敬乾隆九年定議後每遇雨澤稍愆有禱輒應二十四年自春徂
夏望雨迄殷
皇帝稽古定制
却壇乞致屢豐之慶
步禱
皇帝親製祭文行大雩禮先明虔齋由
齋宮步禱
蜀五始齊沛雲四布大祀夕雩霖方施自是連且滂沱田疇沾足會典殷禮攸關敬謹備載
常雩之次以乖永久

上帝前用帛一與

祈穀同樂章燔柴迎

帝神奏需平奠玉帛奏雲平進俎奏需平初獻奏霖平亞獻奏露平終獻奏露平徹饌奏露平送

帝神奏靈平望燎奏需平餘儀均與冬日至大祀同

凡大雩之禮歲孟夏常雩之後如不雨遣官祇告

天神

地祇

太歲越七日不雨告

社稷仍不雨復告

神祇太歲三復不雨遣大雩先祀一日以舉行大雩遣官祇告

太廟是日巳刻

皇帝御常服詣齋宮不作樂不除道不設鹵簿祀日兩冠素服

躬禱於

圜丘設

凡常雩之禮歲以巳月龍見卜日祀

皇乾殿餘儀均與
圜丘同
　皇天上帝於
圜丘為百穀祈膏雨先祀一日
　皇帝齋宿於
南郊詣
　皇穹宇上香詣
圜丘視
壇位
　皇天上帝位
配位
從位均與冬日至大祀同

壇位畢由東門出詣

神庫視籩豆並視牲牢畢廻詣

齋宮祀日設

皇帝拜位於第一成

殿門內設讚祝受福胙位於拜位之前

皇帝由祈年門左門入陞左階進

殿左門至拜位行禮陪祀王公位殿外第一成階上文武百官位第三成階下禮部尚書率太常官詣

皇乾殿恭請

神位安奉

祈年殿

上帝前用帛一樂章燔柴迎

帝神奏祈平奠玉帛奏綏平進俎奏萬平初獻奏寶平亞獻奏穰平終獻奏瑞平徹饌奏渥平送

帝神奏滋平望燎奏穀平禮成禮部尚書率太常官恭請

神位還御

祈年歲以月正上辛祀

上帝為民祈穀

皇天上帝位第一成殿中南嚮奉

太祖高皇帝

太宗文皇帝

世祖章皇帝

聖祖仁皇帝

世宗憲皇帝配饗東西嚮先祀一日

・皇帝詣

南郊齋宿至

祈穀壇外壝南門右降贊引太常卿二人恭導

皇帝入祈年門左門詣

皇乾殿上香行禮詣・

祈年殿恭視

遣官跪贊上香遣官上柱香次三上瓣香與贊復位引遣官自西階降復位贊跪叩興以下升
上帝位前司帛官跪奉篚遣官跪受篚奠於案司爵官跪奉爵遣官跪受爵恭獻奠正中與司視詣祝行禮皆有贊
案前跪三叩奉祝版跪案左贊引遣官由第一成午階右降至第二成讀祝拜位北面跪遣官行三叩禮廻奠帛行初獻禮司帛官奉篚司爵官奉爵以次進遣官升壇詣
司視讀祝畢詣
神位前跪安於案叩如初退遣官行三叩禮仍降西階復位次亞獻奠爵於左次終獻奠爵於右儀並
同廻送
神遣官行三跪九叩禮有司奉祝帛次香恭送燎所遣官轉立拜位西旁東面候過復位引詣內壇
南右門外瘞燎位瘞燎告禮成引由外壇南右門出太常卿率所屬恭請
神位還御皆退
凡祈穀之禮於
南郊
圜丘之北為壇三成上覆以
殿曰

皇帝至昭亨門外陞禮輿大駕鹵簿前導迎樂作奏祐平之章

皇帝回鑾王公從各官以次退不陪祀王公百官仍朝服於

午門外跪迎

午門鳴鐘王公隨

駕入至內金水橋恭候

皇帝還宮各退〇因事祗告遣官將事五鼓太常寺設青幄於

圜丘雞初鳴遣官恭詣於

昭亨門外太常卿率所屬恭奉

皇天上帝神位安奉幄內陳帛一尊一爵三鑪一鐙二薦鹿脯鹿醢兔醢果五品不設牲俎不奏樂贊

引太常贊禮郎二人引遣官入

昭亨門右門由外壝南右門詣

圜丘升自西階至第三成午階上拜位前北而立典儀官贊執事官各供職

官引遣官就拜位立廸迎 以下自迎神至望燎皆典儀官唱贊贊引

神司香官奉香盤進贊引官贊升壇引遣官由西階升至第一成香案前司香官跪奉香贊引官贊跪

皇帝詣飲福受胙拜位立侍衛二人進立於左奉福胙官降立於右

皇帝跪左右執事官咸跪右官進福酒

皇帝受爵拱舉授左官進胙亦如之三拜興復位率羣臣行三跪九拜禮徹饌奏熙平之章有

司詣

上帝位前奉蒼璧退送

帝神奏清平之章

皇帝率羣臣行三跪九拜禮有司奉祝次帛次饌次香恭送燎所

皇帝轉立拜位旁西嚮候祝帛過復位

從位香帛均由東西階奉送至各燎鑪奏太平之章

祝帛燎半奏望燎恭導

皇帝由內壝南左門出至望燎位望燎引分獻官各詣左右門外望燎奏禮成恭導

皇帝由外壝南左門出入大次更衣禮部尚書率太常官恭請

神位還御

皇穹宇

皇帝跪獻爵奠正中興退就讀祝拜位立司祝至祝案前跪三叩奉祝版跪案左樂暫止

皇帝跪羣臣皆跪司祝讀祝畢奉祝版詣

上帝位前跪安於案三叩退樂作

皇帝率羣臣行三拜禮興詣

配位前以次獻爵儀同贊禮郎引分獻官由東西階升壇各詣

從位前上香奠帛以次獻爵畢降階退立原位樂止武功之舞退文舞八佾進行亞獻禮奏嘉平之

章舞羽籥之舞

皇帝陞

壇以次獻爵奠於左儀如初獻復位行終獻禮奏永平之章 舞與亞獻同

皇帝陞

壇以次獻爵奠於右儀如亞獻復位分獻官獻爵均如初樂止文德之舞退太常官贊

賜福胙光祿卿二人就東案奉福胙進至

上帝位前拱舉

皇帝跪受篚奠玉帛興以次詣

列聖配位前奠帛儀同

皇帝復位廸進俎

皇帝轉立拜位旁西嚮有司貯羮於壺恭執自壇下陞午階升詣

上帝位

皇帝復位奏咸平之章

列聖位前各跪拱舉興以羮沃俎者三皆退由西階降

皇帝陞

壇詣

上帝位

配位前跪進俎興復位行初獻禮司爵官各奉爵進奏壽平之章舞干戚之舞

皇帝陞

壇詣

上帝位前司爵官跪進爵

皇帝就拜位立廼燔柴迎
帝神司香官各奉香盤進司樂官贊舉迎
帝神樂奏始平之章 凡舉樂皆司樂
官唱贊後同 贊引官奏陞
壇恭導
皇帝詣第一成
上帝位前司香官跪進香贊引官奏跪
皇帝跪奏上香
皇帝上柱香次三上瓣香興以次詣
列聖配位前上香儀同贊引官奏復位
皇帝復位贊引官奏跪拜興 凡陞壇復位行
禮均有奏後同
皇帝行三跪九拜禮王公百官均隨行禮司玉帛官各奉篚進奏景平之章
皇帝陞
壇詣
上帝位前司玉帛官跪進篚

齋宮陪祀王公百官咸采服分班集

齋宮門外恭候

皇帝入逈退視日日出前七刻太常卿詣

齋宮告時

皇帝御祭服乘禮輿出降輿乘輦鑾儀衞校鳴

齋宮鐘

皇帝至外壇南門外神路右降輦贊引太常卿二人恭導入大次禮部尚書率太常官詣

皇穹宇恭請

神位安奉青幄畢太常卿奏請行禮

皇帝出大次盥洗贊引太常卿恭導

皇帝出外壇南左門入內壇南左門陛午階至二成黃幄次拜位前立太常贊禮郎引分獻官四人由

南右門入至階前夾甬道立鴻臚官引陪祀諸王貝勒位第三階上貝子公位階下百官位外

壇門外左右序立均北面典儀官贊樂舞生登歌執事官各共廼職望燎省饌官唱贊武舞八

佾進贊引官奏就位

駕發警蹕。

午門鳴鐘。大駕鹵簿前導不陪祀王公文武各官咸朝服跪送導迎鼓吹設而不作鑾儀衞校鳴齋宮鐘。

皇帝入壇西門至

昭亨門外降輦贊引太常卿二人恭導

皇帝由左門入詣

皇穹宇於

上帝

列聖前上香畢行三跪九拜禮兩廡

從位遣分獻官上香行禮。

皇帝詣

圜丘視。

壇位詣

神庫視籩豆並視牲牢畢由內壇南左門出外壇南左門。至神路右陞輦詣大明夜明均帛一牛一登一籩豆各十尊二爵三瓚二鑪一鐙二。

星辰帛十有一。

雲雨風雷帛四均牛一羊一豕一登一鉶二籩豆各十尊一爵二瓚二十鑪一鐙二玉帛實於篚牲載於俎尊寶酒疏布冪勺具先祀一日樂部設中和韶樂於壇下分左右懸鑾儀衛陳大駕鹵簿於

午門外玉簮於

太和門階下巳刻太常卿詣

乾清門奏請

皇帝詣齋宮

皇帝御龍袍袞服乘禮輿出宮前引內大臣十人後扈內大臣二人豹尾班執槍佩刀侍衛二十人佩弓矢侍衛二十人翊衛如儀至

太和門階下降輿乘輦

世宗憲皇帝配以

大明

夜明

星辰

雲雨風雷從祀。

上帝位第一成南嚮。

列聖東西嚮。

四從位第二成。

大明西嚮。

星辰在其次。

夜明東嚮。

雲雨風雷在其次均設青幄。

上帝蒼璧一帛十有二犢一登一簠二簋二籩豆各十有二尊一爵三鑪一鐙六爉牛一。

列聖均帛一犢一登一簠簋各二籩豆各十有二尊一爵三鑪一鐙四。

欽定大清會典卷之三十七

　禮部

　　祠祭清吏司

　　　大祀一

　　　　凡郊

天之禮兆陽位於

南郊圜以象

天曰

圜丘。其制三成。歲以冬日至祀

皇天上帝。奉

太祖高皇帝

太宗文皇帝

世祖章皇帝

聖祖仁皇帝

IN COMPLIANCE WITH CURRENT
COPYRIGHT LAW
OCKER & TRAPP INC.
AND
PRINCETON UNIVERSITY
PRODUCED THIS REPLACEMENT VOLUME
ON WEYERHAEUSER COUGAR OPAQUE NATURAL PAPER,
THAT MEETS ANSI/NISO STANDARDS Z39.48-1992
TO REPLACE THE IRREPARABLY
DETERIORATED ORIGINAL. 2001

www.ingramcontent.com/pod-product-compliance
Lightning Source LLC
Chambersburg PA
CBHW030410170426
43202CB00010B/1559